101 Most Am

2016 Guide
to Great Shopping and Retailtainment

101 Most Amazing Stores in New York

2016 Guide
to Great Shopping and Retailtainment

Dorothy B. Polak

INTERMUNDIA ✇ PUBLISHING

Book Design: MPC Graphic Studio
Photographs: Dorothy B. Polak
Technical Editor: Elizabeth Dixon
Copy Editor: Kenward M. Polak

Published by
Intermundia Publishing
New York, info@nowyjorker.com

Second Edition

ISBN-13: 978-1516961733
ISBN-10: 1516961730

3 4 5 6 7 8 9 10
Printed in the United States of America

TABLE OF CONTENTS

MIDTOWN EAST

UPPER EAST SIDE

STORES BY CATEGORY

8

JEWELRY

LINGERIE

TOYS

WITCHCRAFT

Brothers and sisters M&M's, let's brace ourselves, the tourists are coming!

PREFACE

All the stores described in this guide have been chosen not because of brand popularity (or rarity), retail space size, the widest selection of high-quality products, great service, or even the best deals in the city—but because of their capacity for "retailtainment." The term was coined by George Ritzer in 1999, and it is a combination of two words: "retail" and "entertainment."According to him, it is "use of ambience, emotion, sound, and activity to get customers interested in the merchandise and in a mood to buy." As there are always "improvers" of everything, including words and phrases, you can come across some other terms, such as "inspirational retailing," "entertailing," or "shopping experience."

No matter how we call that phenomenon, it has become an important marketing strategy, helping to build brand recognition and popularity as well as bringing customers to stores through providing them with both superior commodities and various fun (often interactive) activities. This makes their shopping experience one-of-a-kind, multisensory and multilevel entertainment—not available anywhere else, particularly in all those cookie-cutter chain stores. This little guide, by nature, is highly selective and arbitrary; it contains the descriptions of 100 most retailtaining stores in Manhattan only (often called "the city," also in this guide).

The author, Dorothy B. Polak, an art historian by profession, did her best to present not only the most amusing retail outlets but also the most beautiful because of their distinctive interior design. The layout of the guide is very perspicuous so that tourists can easily find necessary information or compile their own must-see list taking advantage of the alphabetical and subject indexes and visual elements, such as maps, graphic symbols.

It may happen that after publishing this guide some of the stores described in it will change, let's say, their décor or inventory, or location, or even name. If so, please don't be disappointed. It happens all the time, especially in such a dynamic place as Manhattan. After all, everything here lasts a New York minute. Happy shopping…

FINANCIAL DISTRICT AND TRIBECA

Lower Manhattan from the southern tip of the city to Canal Street is one of the most popular (which means crowded) tourist destinations because of the density of must-see attractions—probably the highest in the entire city. Even though there are fewer stores than landmarks and museums per square mile here, Financial District is also one of the city's best shopping destinations. Among main tourist/consumer attractions are the Century 21 bargain store, Brookfield Place, and other retail outlets of famous brands. They are all located in the rows of the city's oldest townhouses in the Sea Port area. Near TriBeCa there are many designer boutiques for shoppers with well-stuffed wallets or just visitors.

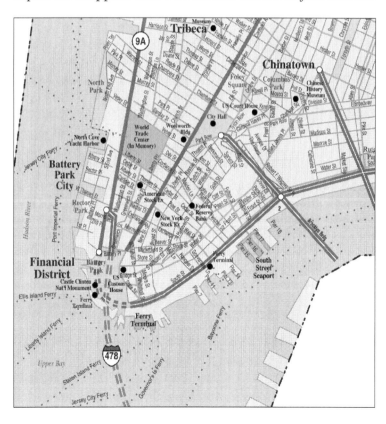

The last of the Mohicans in Manhattan by the entrance of Western Spirit

Brookfield Place

220 Vesey Street
www.brookfieldplace.ny
🚊Subway directions:
Cortland Street (1)

Memory was the first to come to WTC Plaza, where once the Twin Towers overlooked the entire city before the 9/11 attacks. Now this place is vibrant with zingy New York life. The landscape of this area has changed significantly, especially owing to the Freedom Tower, the tallest building in the USA. In its immediate vicinity is the 9/11 Memorial Museum.

The place again is full of stores and restaurants, mush-rooming here all the time, among which is reigns supreme the legendary department store Century 21, having survived the 9/11 tragedy. So, everything here looks almost the same as it was before the harrowing 2001 attacks on the World Trade Center, and for that reason, this "almost" brings tears to the eyes of both New Yorkers and the visitors.

Near the place, where once the Twin Towers stood, the Winter Garden also miraculously survived though all the palms and other plants in it and its glass structure suffered the same fate as the human 9/11 victims. Luckily, the shopping mall survived as well. After 13 years of extensive restoration, the site with its beautiful atrium and Brookfield Place Shopping Center opened in April 2015. This time, the popular chain stores, which operated here before, have been replaced by up-scale designer boutiques of Hermes, Burberry Diane von Furstenberg, Saks off Fifth (the only other location of Saks outside Fifth Avenue), to name a few. It looks as if the place aspires to become one a Fifth Avenue clone and another luxury shopping mecca of the city. In the space around the Garden Atrium, there are over a dozen restaurants and grocery stores, including the classy Le District offering French-inspired gourmet food.

All this luxury goes very well with the monumental granite architecture of this place: the glass atrium with the view of the

Hudson river, and a life-size palm grove under the ten-story high glass dome.

The shopping mall hosts theatrical, musical, and art events as Brookfield Place is not only a shopping mall in a historic building but also a cultural center with its concert hall, stage, museum, and small sculpture park with the art installation, "The Real World," created by one of the most famous artists in the city, Tom Otterness.

By the way, the sculptures are based on a motif of a penny go exceptionally well with luxury shopping.

Recently several new stores have opened in the area, and most of them represent luxury brands. Another shopping center in WTC Plaza, Westfield Underground Mall, hosting about 150 stores, situated in a new transit hub space, opens in the second half of 2015. It was planned as a kind of replica of the stores operated here before the 9/11. Like Brookfield Place, it will mostly sell luxury goods of such brands as Kiehl's, L'Occitane, Miachel Kors, Tom Ford, La Colomba, and many others. All this in in the marble maze, stretching for many miles. Impressive!

These two up-scale shopping centers revive Lower Manhattan for us, and make it even more tourist- and customer-friendly than it ever has been. It is a serious competition for Fifth and Madison Avenues.

Duane Reade
100 Broadway (at Pine Street)
www.duanereade.com
🚇Subway directions:
Wall Street (4, 5)

What makes a chain drugstore interesting besides the fact it is the largest in the entire city? The answer is—its style. Duane Reade pharmacy at Broadway and Pine Street is, in fact, the biggest and the most elegant of all Duane Reade stores in the city, occupying a historic building space of 22,000 square feet.

It opened in July 2012 and became an instant landmark in the revitalized post-9/11 neighborhood.

Why is this specific Duane Reade worth visiting not only as a pharmacy but also as a tourist attraction? Mainly because of the "museum factor," specifically a permanent museum-style exhibit arranged in the entire store space, presenting the history of the vicinity of the world-famous Wall Street, accompanied by the display of US history events that affected this part of the city and Broadway itself.

However, this two-story emporium is not about the past, but mostly about the busy present, by the counters and stands on the main floor—creatively arranged under the antique golden stucco ceiling propped with Corinthian columns.

And, of course, there are a pharmacy department and Express RX kiosks to dispense refills quickly, located on the mezzanine with the finely wrought metal balustrade.

The assortment of drugs and cosmetics is the same as in other Duane Reade outlets, but the food court is really unique, including an up-market gourmet salad bar, a juice bar taking customized orders, a cafe with a professional barista, and a row of self-serve machines selling soups and frozen yoghourt in the middle of the first floor. There is a sushi bar here, too.

The store, operating in a busy tourist destination in Lower Manhattan, also offers the largest and most comprehensive selection of Papyrus greeting cards, referring to the old American tradition of drugstores, where, apart from Aspirin, cough syrup, and soda straight from the fountain at the counter, you can buy almost everything 24/7.

Century 21 Department Store

22 Cortland Street (between Broadway and Trinity Place)
www.c21stores.com
🚇Subway directions:
Cortland Street (N, R)
Fulton Street (4, 5, A, C, J, Z)

Century 21 Department Store is one of the good examples of an open secret despite it is advertised as "the best-kept secret in the city." Both New Yorkers and tourists fill the store in crowds every day. Although it occupies six floors and a huge space, it's never easy to squeeze between the aisles—shoppers are everywhere, but even if you are claustrophobic, the place is worth visiting, anyway. They are lured here by the above-mentioned slogan and the fact that it still is the first on the New York's shrinking list of so-called "bargain stores."

Undoubtedly, it owes its popularity also to its location—just near the 9/11 Memorial at the site of World Financial Center.

As psychology and social science have proved, what we love about shopping is—shopping. In other words, not the result is important, but the very process; that is, choosing, comparing, taking off the shelves, touching, and eventually, trying on. And of course, those shivers down our spines when we hunt for bargains.

Probably, it's an atavism after our prehistoric ancestors who went plucking berries and hunting for mammoths. That's why, rummaging and browsing through shelves filled with garments, lingerie, accessories, jewelry, cosmetics, shoes, household appliances, kitchenware, towels … is so enjoyable.

All this is like that hunted down mammoth in caveman times—only this time a signature shopping bag filled with an Armani 75% off is a trophy and a proof of successful hunting. The satisfaction is even higher as all the merchandise in Century 21 is a real bargain of well-known brands, including Prada, Jacobs, Galliano, Chanel. And it's always guaranteed, no exceptions allowed.

Bowne & Co Stationers

211 Water Street (between Fulton and Beekman Streets)
www.seany.org
🚇Subway directions:
Fulton Street (2, 3)
Fulton Street (A, C, J, Z)
Wall Street (2, 3)

Bowne & Co Stationers occupies the main floor in a historic townhouse at the cobblestone street, leading to one of the city's most crowded tourist attractions—Sea Port. It is a stationery shop that can be easily mistaken for a small printmaking museum, mostly because of the antique interior with the dark beam ceiling, the old-timbered floor, wooden shelves, cabinets, display tables, and, before anything else, antique printmaking equipment.

Although it is not the original place where Robert Bowne, a Quaker, established his store nearby on Pearl Street in 1775, the memorabilia of its long history, placed throughout the shop, don't allow to forget about the past of Bowne & Co.

A short travel through time reminds customers that the novelties, such as paper cases, envelopes, postal cards and paper pads and chalks, were introduced to New Yorkers by Bowne & Co itself.

You can visit the store and buy custom-made invitations printed on an antique letterpress, greeting cards, vintage paper toys, posters, journals, blank books, notepads and limited-edition volumes in multiple nineteenth-century styles.

The store also takes orders for personalized paperwork of all types and prints. All this is done of on antique hand presses, including the thoroughly restored Columbian one. Visiting this place is a perfect source of creative New York gifts acquired on an unforgettable and nostalgic travel through time—a free history lesson included.

Harley Davidson of NYC

374-378 Broadway (between White and Franklin Streets)
www.nycharleydavidson.com
🚇Subway directions:
Canal Street (J, N, Q, R, Z, 6)

William Harley and the brothers Davidson made the first Harley-Davidson bike in Milwaukee (Wisconsin) in 1903, but it immediately became an icon of New York as the symbol of innovation, enterprise, courage, and freedom. Who, nowadays, saying "Harley-Davidson" associates it with Milwaukee?

As befits a cult brand, it has had its showroom in Manhattan since forever. Once it was in Midtown, but it moved to its current TriBeCa location at the beginning of 2014.

The newest HD flagship, occupying the two levels of an 12 000-square-foot space, exclusively designed by the renowned architect Sean Karns, is worthy of its name both because of its design and latest technologies. Its facade is predominantly made of glass, and its interior's red-brick walls, "urban," metal structural elements and furnishings joining glass with raw wood emphasize and define the brand.

The showroom fits perfectly to New York context, which is enhanced by large-size photographs of local architectural landmarks. The lower level even more so simulates the "New York spirit" because the latest models of Harley Davidson are displayed on a gray resin flooring, which resembles a real garage in the city. The metal platform called "Glass Bike Lift," suspended from the ceiling by thick chains, which moving in the glass shift in a Hollywood style, completes the picture, and materializes Harley bikers' desires by transporting cult motorcycles to happy customers.

Being the newest of all brand showrooms, it's packed with all possible technical novelties, especially a unique movie-theater-size screen, called Harley-Davidson Powerball. It displays the prototypes of bikes designed by customers in multi-touch kiosks. You can only imagine how much fun it is. And it is not just that—customers can implement their designs on the spot. Their bikes can be exactly as they were dreamed of. This is also the only store in the world where you can buy the absolutely latest models of HD. The showroom offers a spectacular selection of bike accessories, gadgets, leather jackets, T-shirts, among others.

After so many impressions, customers can have coffee in the café just at the entrance, and over a cup of freshly brewed Arabica, dream of the intoxicating aroma of gas, listening to a pleasurable roar of bike engines. Who knows, if you visit the store, maybe you'll fall in love with a Harley-Davidson bike—this metal Cyclops glowering at you and whispering sweetly "take me, take me...." Indeed, it's really hard to imagine something more, by nature, resembling Manhattan.

Western Spirit
395 Broadway (between White Street and Walker Street)
www.westernspirit.com
🚆Subway directions:
Canal Street (N, R, Q, 4, 6)

Everybody probably remembers from "The Midnight Cowboy" that cowboys are rather unwelcome visitors in New York City, except for one who seems to be more New Yorky than any other buckaroo. He performs as a street artist in Times Square, "clothed" only in a hat, boots, and a guitar.

Western Spirit, one of only a few stores in the city selling cowboy gear, is located far from the Times Square cowboy, in the heart of Chinatown (although there is nothing made in China in it). Before you enter this temple of the Wild West, you will see a life-size wooden figure of an Indian chief bearing all the adequate clothing attributes and props.

After you have already come inside, you will see hundreds (if not thousands) of items, filling almost completely the spacious interior of the store, coming from local manufacturers or handmade by Native Americans, of course, everything in western-spirit tradition

Many tourists seem to be more interested in sightseeing the place than eventually buying something. No wonder a big-letter sign at the entrance says that everything in here is for sale. So even a stuffed armadillo and a longhorn bull's skull, are not just exhibits. The store inventory includes complete cowboy outfits in many different styles, including a wide selection of original boots of all sizes, broad-brimmed Stetsons, chaparajos (leather riding leggings), and rodeo fringe shirts, to name a few. To make the "Wild West" experience even more exciting, there are also authentic Navajo headdresses, quilts, arrows, and suchlike items in here. However, in Western Spirit, there are not only western-movie-style props, but also different items from the first half of the 20th century, for instance, "almost authentic" Coca Cola memorabilia.

If you are tired after many hours of sightseeing, your feet will be grateful for buying a pair of well-fitting moccasins hand-made by Native Americans.

J.Crew Liquor Store

235 W Broadway (between White and Walker Streets)
www.liquorstoretribeca.com
🚇Subway directions:
Franklin Street (1, 2)
Canal Street (A, C, E)
Canal Street (N, R)

Where do New York men go shopping when they need a new sweater, suit or silk tie? Usually they head for one of the men's garment stores from the latest top ten list.

However, sometimes they visit...a liquor store, or more specifically, the one at the West Broadway location, which a couple of years ago was transformed into J.Crew's menswear-only boutique, still operating under its "inherited" red and blue neon sign blazing: "Liquor Store," and in its just slightly remodeled interior. Inside, everything except for haberdashery is old-style: plush leather chairs, antiquated displays, dark paneling, props and bric-a-brac strewn all over the place, a miniature ship and airplane built from beer cans, opaque liquor bottles (glasses are perfectly clean and transparent), oriental rugs, globetrotter trunks, and a bookshelf crammed with dust-covered classics—from Hemingway to Kerouac and Ginsberg. This old-time atmosphere is completed by almost den-like dim lighting.

Let's not be deceived by appearances—the outlet offers the newest lines of dapper menswear: cashmere cardigans, merino wool sweaters, Borsalino Doria hats and caps, fedoras, chic shoes, jewel-tone ties—more or less formalwear for guys of all guys of all ages and sizes.

If you are a little tired after long hours of touring, you can rest your elbows on the authentic bar counter, but despite all the bottles and glasses, alcohol is not served here. At least, you can nibble on nuts placed in one of the plates.

Tribeca Issey Miyake

119 Hudson Street (at North Moore Street)
www.tribecaisseymiyake.com
🚇Subway directions:
Franklin Street (1, 2)
Canal Street (A, C, E)

It's obvious we go to a clothing store to buy clothing; however, in some cases it's worth visiting them for other reasons, especially if they are so-called concept or flagship stores, which promote themselves in the same way as art museums do, that is to say, by dint of outstanding architecture and interior design.

In fact, some of the most interesting New York stores resemble art galleries where the newest fashion collections are presented as contemporary art exhibitions. It's even more evident when some designers follow avant-garde art as their means of expression as does Issey Miyake, a fashion designer and recognized artist.

That is, probably, the reason why the main and the most spectacular feature of his Tribeca flagship, four-level store is a sculpture by a famous architect and sculptor Frank Gehry. It is a gigantic metal installation called "Voxel," and it's made of hexagonal shapes—voxels, forming three-story, cloud-shaped structure arranged as the upscale honeycomb display spaces—fully interactive and touch-activated.

All around the walls of this stark interior, there are also paintings by Gehry's son—Alejandro. Simple glass display tables and metal racks on wheels are the only pieces of furniture.

The artsy Miyake store is undoubtedly worth visiting, especially if you are a fashionista having a liking for the very avant-garde IM clothing lines. Even if you don't go for that kind of stuff, Gehry's amazing sculpture is worth seeing, and on top of that, you don't have pay any admittance fee, so you can use the saved money to buy one of the iconic signature IM pieces of fashion art, although the price tag can be a little discouraging. However, good art is never cheap.

SOHO AND GREENWICH VILLAGE

Historically, the fragment of the city from Canal to Houston Streets was a district of art galleries. Now this is one of the most popular shopping destinations, jammed with "the big names" boutiques. The narrow streets on both the sides of Broadway have become the new "Madison Avenue." This part of Broadway, with its row of historical "cast and iron" buildings also hosts popular clothing brands, from Top Shop to the gigantic flagship of Adidas on Broadway and Houston Street corner. The smaller streets in the neighborhood are filled with not so big but even more spectacular boutiques of prestigious names—Chanel to Prada and Barney's (Co-op) to Bloomingdale's, and of avant-garde outlets established by the youngest generation of designers, such as Alexander Wang, John Varvatos, among others.

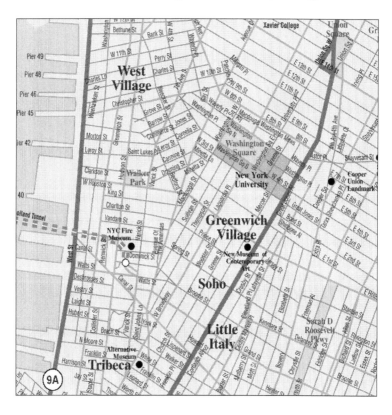

The stairs with words of endearment in Opening Ceremony

Opening Ceremony

33-35 Howard Street (between Crosby Street and Broadway)
www.openingceremony.us
🚇Subway directions:
Canal Street (N, Q, R, J, Z, 6)

In America everybody says "I love you," and strangers greet strangers on the streets with "How are you?"

In Manhattan, not only New Yorkers do so, but even—stairs, especially these leading to the red-painted door on the second floor at 33-35 Howard Street Building in SoHo. The staircase is also red, and its steps greet shoppers with Valenyine's-Day-cards-style phrases such as "Hello. I love you,"Want you tell me your name," "Let me jump in your name," and the likes.

So New Yorkish.

However, not only the love confessing stairs seem to represent the New York state of mind here, but the entire store. All this thanks to the owners of OC, Carol Lim and Humberto Leon and their open attitude to novelties and changes—even avant-garde ones—and their passion for traditional and multicultural exoticism. It's no wonder that nothing in Opening Ceremony, looks twice the same in any season.

To keep faith to this exoticness principle, the owners visit other country every year and pick up the most unusual local items for inspiration. This, among other things, has resulted in designing Havaianas flip-flops—now worn by the entire world.

They like to experiment by giving a chance to budding designers to become famous, as well. The store also cooperates with widely recognized popular brands, but only to create unique lines of products, dedicated specifically for the OC brand.

Opening Ceremony, occupying two town houses with four stories and a basement, is more than just a store—it is something in between a showroom and an art gallery with a designer shop. Moreover, it is the place where people not only can shop but also draw inspiration and socialize under the hangers with fashionable clothes. It's worth mentioning that this store boasts very high standards of interior design, which is one of the best in the city.

Opening Ceremony is a mecca for in-the-know fashionistas from all over Manhattan (and now, thanks to this guide, from all over the world), attracted here by famous avant-garde designers' labels such as Rodarte, Proenza Schouler, or Alexander Wang.

The creative imagination of the owners has made this store both inviting and inspiring. By the way, have you ever seen a pig with a display case on its back (of course, the plastic one)? Or have you bought something under the row of gigantic women legs on high heels, spread right above your head? The answer is probably, "no," so, even if you are not a fashionista, it's worth walking the red love-confessing stairs to take part in an opening ceremony in Opening Ceremony.

Pearl River Mart

477 Broadway (between Broome and Grand Streets)
www.pearlriver.com
🚇Subway directions:
Canal Street (N, R, Q)

Why does everything in New York seem to be cheaper than, say, in London or Paris? Because most merchandise available in Manhattan is made in China.

There are rumors that even such iconic local designers as Ralph Lauren and Calvin Klein cooperate with factories in the Far East, but it's not likely to find this kind of information on their labels (if so, in the finest print).

Thus, instead of spending a fortune on goods that are knockoffs, you can buy genuine Asian products firsthand in Pearl River Mart, where everything is Chinese by definition. Although Chinese New Yorkers are not the largest minority group, only they have their own ethnic department store in China Town (as of this writing, this address is true, but because of ginormous rent hike, the store will move somewhere else in Manhattan, and I will update this).

All the three vast floors and basement offer everything Chinese. No wonder The Village Voice hailed it as "The Best Chinatown Kitsch Superstore in 2012," and it does everything to live up to this opinion.

You can buy here any imaginable and unimaginable items associated with China, including wrappers and kimonos (and other costumes, often of natural silk), kung fu shoes, folk dolls dressed in replicas of national clothes, tableware, natural cosmetics, bamboo trees in elaborate pots, paper lanterns and lampshades, and even dozen-foot-or-so-long crêpe paper dragons for several thousand dollars each.

In one of the corners of the basement is the pharmacy where you can buy traditional medicines (if you are a brave soul), such as potions and ointments made from herbs or some venoms, and teas and unique spices in colorful tins and jars. Gourmets can also be satisfied here with sweets, rice cakes, and food, mostly prepacked rice and noodles as well as delicious Chinese desserts.

The assortment is impressive, and it's really hard to itemize at least the smallest percentage of the inventory. For the curious, I can list a few more: rice paper screens, small waterworks, chandeliers, Buddha figurines, pillows, bamboo furniture (at home décor department), high-tech gadgets, jewelry, such as pearl-incrusted knick-knacks, and even birdcages.

There is simply a bit of everything Chinese here, and, of course, at Chinese prices. At a dollar, or so, apiece, you can buy rubber flip flops, umbrellas (frankly, for use once only), plastic toys.

Pearl River Mart is so huge that staying inside for an hour is just like catching a brief glimpse of its kaleidoscopic interior, shimmering with lustrous rainbow colors, or rather these of pearls. The store's name says it all, and it really is the "genuine" Chinese jewel of Chinatown.

Visiting it is like an exotic travel to the Far East, however much easier on the wallet and much friendlier for the feet.

MoMA Design and Book Store
81 Spring Street (between Broadway and Crosby Street)
www.momastore.com
🚇Subway directions:
5th Avenue/53 Street (E, M)
57th Street (F)
7th Avenue (B, D, E)

Times change, and so does tourism. One of the proofs of these changes is the new generation of museum stores, enabling a tourist to buy museum-style gifts and memorabilia—without visiting the actual museum. This option seems to be invaluable for a modern globetrotter who usually needs to see everything from a "must-see list" and still have enough time for the most important agenda item—shopping. And this brings us to MoMA Design and Book Store.

In fact, this retail outlet in SoHo offers more than the original uptown museum location—besides typical souvenirs (with motifs of the museum's highlights), such as books, postcards, posters, lithographs, p, art supplies, jewelry, and the like, you can also find ultra-modern pieces of furniture, cutting-edge kitchenware, and futuristic home décor gadgets in its inventory.

The very name itself: "museum store," regardless of its distance from the museum, obliges the store to cater for the aesthetic needs and cultural ambitions of customers, even those who haven't been aware of them yet.

Art at its best still will allure visitors from every corner of the store, which is, in fact, a MoMA branch. The store looks like a museum department and operates like one, with just one small exception—to visit it, you don't have to enter any museum at all.

C. Wonder
72 Spring Street (between Lafayette Street and Crosby Streets)
www. cwonder.com
🚇Subway directions:

Spring Street (4, 6)
Prince Street (N, R)
Broadway-Lafayette St (B, D, F, M)

As was once said, "A shopping destination that transports women into a World of luxury and surprises," and that all for mere 50 bucks a piece? If there is something like it in Manhattan, there is—no wonder—C. Wonder!

The flagship store of the C. Wonder retail chain founded and owned by Christopher Burch (ex-husband of Tory) sells women's clothing, accessories and home décor, and not only offers products of outstanding quality and astonishing value but also sells "the setting that excites and inspires."

C. Wonder keeps its promise, at least about the interior arrangement, which is always changing. Its windows and floor displays, gorgeous decorative items and intriguing and resourceful surprises to uncover (announced on the C. Wonder website) making a shopping experience even more pleasant.

The space behind the huge green door, flanked with bright green and white walls (mostly striped) with the brand signature "C" logo pattern almost everywhere, is divided into many small and cozy, boutique-style theme areas full of colorful graphic motifs and stylish props. Such as enormous (six feet, at least) teddy bears covered with flowers and rainbow-striped, full-sized zebras, among others.

The décor is usually coordinated with the vast assortment of merchandise on the shelves. So the kitchen utensils department may look like an original rustic kitchen (Provence style) and a young-fashion aisle—like a high-school girl's room, but as mentioned above, the décor often changes, which makes the place be never twice the same nor boring.

The changes refer also to the "monogram parlor" (an aisle dedicated to personalize by monogramming everything—from pillows to mugs), and to the classic Vespa motorbike standing in the very middle of the space; at one time, it may be all pink, at another—covered with roses. All the arrangements are surprisingly creative and most of them also funny, making shopping here a real pleasure and fun. And—as promised—all that luxury is usually under 50 bucks, so every customer could feel him- or herself like Alice in (C.)Wonderland.

Evolution Store
120 Spring Street (between Mercer Street and Green Street)
www.theevolutionstore.com
🚇Subway directions:
Prince Street (N, R)
Spring Street (4, 6,)
Broadway-Lafayette Street (B, D, F, M)

Since more than half of Americans do not believe in evolution, it's obvious they need an evolution store. And they have it. However, for some reasons, the one and only shop of this kind in US and probably in the entire world is operating in the city which needs it least, so to say—in New York. The reason is simple: living here means the acceptance of social Darwinism as a rule, or—moving to New Jersey.

The skeleton, greeting guests at the entrance, is just the beginning of a long and fascinating evolution lesson in the two story townhouse with the interior that looks like the small version of a natural history museum,. Unlike With that just difference from the original one in Upper West Side, that everything here is not only possible to touch, but also to take home.

Besides skeletons of all sizes, the store offers fossils and hundred-thousand-year-old bones (not necessary authentic, of course), taxidermy lynx and other stuffed animals, dried bats under the glass domes and such bestsellers of all time as jewel beetle earrings or the raccoon penis in a glass vial.

The inventory includes beetles in glass cases, preserved ugly frogs and beautiful butterflies, hideous spiders and their incredibly elegant webs pressed in the glass, jolly grasshoppers and dangerous scorpions, rare seashells and common insects, as well.

The store is like a biology geek's dream come true. And since seeing is believing, even after a short visit here some skeptics of Darwinian theory may eventually convert to ardent believers in evolution.

Balenciaga

148 Mercer Street (between Houston and Prince Streets)
www.balenciaga.com
🚇Subway directions:
Prince Street (N, R)

Paris in New York? No problem. Just arrive in SoHo, where, at 148 Mercer Street, a new flagship store came into existence in 2014. It looks very modern, even avant-garde, but ,as one of its creators once said, "It draws inspiration from the historical heart of the House at 10 Avenue George V."

Why is this specific address so important for this boutique? Because it was the place of Cristóbal Balenciaga's atelier. He was an outstanding designer, who founded the world-famous Balenciaga Fashion House.

That's why, for the new art director of the brand Alexander Wang and the interior designer Ryan Korban, it was very important to hark back to the "artistic DNA" established by Cristobal Balenciaga. They have chosen Italian marble verde rammeggiatto (which means "green and venose") for the store's interior design, so now the entire boutique is greenish and veiny—the floor and walls, and even furniture.

The only thing that is not marble here is the ceiling, made of glass panels creating a huge window with a view of the Manhattan sky.

To replace the typical SoHo townhouse roof with clear glass was a brilliant idea, the interior brings to mind a planetarium or studio of an Italian renaissance painter. Without this ceiling, it would look like a Florentine graveyard chapel. The associations of the store with art are quite justifiable since, in most instances, the Balenciaga garments are not only pieces of fashion art but also pieces of art itself. That is why, considering the boutique's interior and its merchandise, it is more of an art gallery than a store. The Manhattan sky above the shopppers' heads and Manhattan sky-high prices make us likely to watch and admire the collections rather than to buy them.

Besides, why not feel for twenty minutes or so as a New Yorker in Paris?

Longchamp

132 Spring Street (between Greene & Wooster Streets)
www.us.longchamp.com
🚇Subway directions:
Prince Street (N, R)

Some people say that the "curse of Guggenheim" has made a stairway the second architectural symbol of New York, following skyscrapers, of course. After all, one of Manhattan's nicknames is Skyscraper National Park. However, it is stairways that form the so-called New York style, and no matter whether a building is two- or one-hundred-story-high, it has a spectacular white staircase, preferably Guggenheimesque, or at least a spiral one.

Even stores in the most expensive sites, where every cubic inch of retail space is worth a fortune, have to show off more or less impressive stairs. Among the most spectacular ones are the stairway in Armani store at Fifth Avenue (on page 117 in this guide), Hermes at Madison (page 139) and Prada in SoHo (page 43). However, none of them bears comparison with the Longchamp store that seems to be—all stairs, a creation of the famous British designer Thomas Haetherwick, called the Leonardo da Vinci of our times.

This amazing staircase consolidates the store's entire space, serving as a central point of the whole three-story building and as a display and trading area of the French-based Longchamp brand flagship, offering mostly bags and luxury leather accessories.

The building in which Longchamp is located, after an extensive renovation, in 2006, won many awards for the highest achievement in architecture and was hailed as La Mason Unique (French for "unique home"). All the accolade was bestowed on the store mostly because of the outstanding staircase, which looks like a mountain waterfall: the stairs "fall down" from the glass ceiling towards the floor like a water cascade. It is so large that only one third of all the space is available for the business itself. Having seen that, it's hard to imagine any better space for selling Longchamp's merchandise.

To complete the experience of being in this one-of-a-kind store, you can buy Zip bag, designed exclusively for Longchamp by Thomas Heatherwick himself. It costs several hundred dollars, as almost everything here. Fortunately, the staircase is free—to see and step on, which is really priceless.

Kiki de Montparnasse

79 Greene Street (between Broome and Spring Streets)
www.kikidm.com
🚉Subway directions:
Spring Street (C, E)
Prince Street (N, R)

This upscale boutique offering lingerie and "bed time" accessories, named after Kiki de Montparnasse (the muse of Man Ray, one of the most famous founders of surrealism), was open in 1940. And since noblesse oblige, this place is not just another fancy lingerie store but rather a busy art gallery with all the items from temporary exhibitions for sale at affordable prices. In fact, it looks neither like a retail shop nor like an art parlor because both the display windows and the store interior resemble an elegant, so to say, demimondaine ladies' home.

The entire inventory of this refined and at the same time frivolous silk and lace lingerie, bras, nighties, signature body cosmetics, brand silk linen and so-called "instruments of pleasure" (which means—bedroom toys like famous golden handcuffs and tuxedo boy pants) are arranged within the space remaining a French style boudoir.

This luxurious and sensual atmosphere is created with plush drapes, classy dark wood cabinets, shelves and case displays, wooden wall paneling with nude-art photographs all over, "lust" soft sofas and elegant, wood and glass furniture (with even more nude photo albums to browse). There is even a sleep-ready bed covered with silk bedding at the back of the store, and fitting rooms with three types of lit signs –"before, during and after."

In this voluptuous environment, even a leather whip looks like a precious piece of art and a perfect gift from Gotham City, with love.

Burton Snowboard Store

106 Spring Street (between Mercer and Green Streets)
www.burton.com
🚊Subway directions:
Prince Street (N, R)
Spring Street (4, 6)
Broadway-Lafayette Street (B, D, F, M)

In winter, there are many skating rinks throughout the city, including the most famous one at Rockefeller Center Plaza and these in Central Park and Bryant Park. However, in New York, even in the middle of hot summer months, there is always a place to cool down.

One of the best ideas to do so is just to plunge into the Burton Snowboard flagship store with the world-recognized winter sports gear. The fun factor is not only about the atmosphere but also the so-called "experience" for winter sports lovers.

Burton Snowboard has no ski slopes inside; however, it has a "cool room" (extreme minus temperatures) at the back of the store to test warmth of the clothes in real ski resort conditions. The interior is furnished with a lot of wooden everything.

Some of the fixtures are made of original chairlift parts to recreate the atmosphere of an old-time ski resort, somewhere on the top of a snowy mountain.

Being in the middle of Manhattan in the 21st century, there are huge LCD screens with winter theme clips and photos everywhere.

So the past is present here mostly in a century-old accents, such as an olden blackboard in the window, informing where in the world it is snowing today.

Crocs

143 Spring Street (at Wooster Street corner)
www.crocks.com/ny/soho
🚇Subway directions:
Spring Street (N, R)

To tell the truth, New Yorkers, especially those from Manhattan, do not consider themselves the biggest fans of Crocs. The primary problem they have with these distinctive foam shoes is not that they are flat, bulky and rather unsophisticated, but their color. They are far from black and grey, the only shades defining a true local taste.

Anyway, the store is one of the most fascinating in Manhattan. It opened in a thoroughly restored two-century-old landmark townhouse.

The long renovation of this three-story previous residence came consisted in the reconstruction of the historic façade and bold structural alterations at the back of the building, including the replacement of the brick walls with modern transition glass pieces. Inside the store the original gambrel roof was lifted, and its steel rafter weathered framing was exposed. In this part of the store, there are minimalist white shelves with countless pairs of beige and white crock shoes neighboring the original red brick walls.

In this place, history meets modernity, and even bright-colored foam Crocs footwear seems to look classier, though for tourists who, after long hours of sight-seeing, came across this pink and yellow comfort kingdom, it may be the least important shoe feature.

Sabon

123 Prince Street (between Greene and Wooster Streets)
www.sabonnyc.com
🚊Subway directions:
Prince Street (N, R)
Broadway-Lafayette Streets (B, D, F, M)
Spring Street (A, C, E)

This famous top-brand retail chain for "soapholics" has a few other locations throughout Manhattan, offering almost the same assortment of high-quality body products, soaps, lotions, salts, scrubs and every imaginable product of this kind.

However, the flagship Sabon store in SoHo, as expected, is the most glorious of all the brand chain outlets because of its extensive inventory. This gloriousness is completed by the store's interior with wooden floors, old library-style cabinets and shelves jam-packed with jars and boxes filled with arcane potions and scents.

A handcrafted, Jerusalem stone sink, looking more like an antique atrium fountain in the very center of the store, surrounded by countless soap samples to try on the spot, literally promising "a luxurious experience not to be missed, "especially in a hot summer day in the middle of Manhattan.

This hidden city oasis with its wide selection of soap everything, cool interior and relaxing atmosphere is like a lavender field (or, whatever scent you prefer) in the heart of Manhattan.

RRL (Double Ralph Lauren)

379 West Broadway (between Broome and Spring Streets)
www.ralphlauren.com
🚊Subway directions:
Spring Street (A, C, E)

It must be a coincidence that the RRL store opened on Broadway West, but, at the same time, it shows that even coincidences are not quite coincidental.

Oddly enough, this retail outlet, offering the Wild West garments, shoes, and accessories for present-day aficionados of cowboy style, opened in the location named "west."
Besides the Naked Cowboy, a street performer on Times Square, there are no genuine cowboys in New York nowadays. They all moved to the West a long time ago and never came back, so cowboys' legends no longer belong to the American East heritage and identity.

However, western spirit and looks are still present, at least in RRL on West Broadway, represented by cowboy boots and hats, blue jeans, flannel shirts and leather vests, among others things.

This legendary American west was brought to New York by one of the most famous American designers of our times, Ralph Lauren, who usually is not associated with western inspirations but rather traditional high-society English elegance and the iconic preppy look. But cowboys?

Although he was raised in New York, by designing the RRL store, he has revealed his western nature. Moreover, he is the owner of a several-hundred-acre ranch in Colorado and is a big fan of cowboy way of life, and, of course, cowboy attire. You've guessed it, he collects everything from the Wild West.

It is not surprising he has turned a typical retail space into a western-style store, with a creaking wooden floor, a leather club sofa, antique display cabinets, wide counters, and olden cash boxes. Even lighting, mirrors, books, sepia photographs, hat stands, and other props of the setting recreate the feeling of the times when cowboys, gold diggers and crowds of settlers wore blue denims. By the way, Oscar Wilde allegedly once said that westerners were the best-dressed men in America.

Maybe only for that reason, Ralph Lauren has decided to open this kind of store not somewhere in Los Angeles, but in SoHo, one of the most influential fashion districts in Manhattan, where being well-dressed is definitely not enough.

McNally Jackson Bookstore

52 Prince Street (at Mulberry and Lafayette Streets, Nolita)
www.mcnallyjackson.com
🚇Subway directions:
Spring Street (6)
Broadway-Lafayette Street (B, D, F)

A cup of coffee or tea, and a comfortable antique chair, next to the shelves full of books and magazines is not a typical bookstore's experience—but really appreciated during a busy tourist day in Manhattan. You can sit here for a while, rest, read, or just contemplate whatever you like.

McNally Jackson Bookstore is the independent venture of a large Canadian chain, owned by the founders' daughter Sarah McNally, who started her family business far from home.

And in New York, Nolita (a part of Littlle Italy), she opened a small (in comparison to Barnes&Noble, with "only" some 55,000 titles in stock), but wisely organized "by geography" bookstore with the "local atmosphere," so appreciated by New Yorkers.

Its unique style is emphasized by a café bar inside, walls entirely covered with book pages, lamp shades made from piles of hardcovers, cozy chaise-longues arranged all around the two-story space, photographs and paintings hanging everywhere as in an art gallery, and live plants, to complete the picture.

But wait, there's more.

The store serves a one-of-a-kind Espresso in the city. In this case, "Espresso" stands for the city's first and only Espresso Book Machine, which can print and bind "on demand" any public-domain book (some seven million copies) or a book written by you and brought here in pdf format.

All the above-mentioned in-store attractions, an extensive selection of highly readable books, and weekly events with people worth listening to and discussing with make this place exceptional.

MiN Apothecary and Atelier

117 Crosby Street (between Prince and Jersey Streets)
www.minnewyork.com
🚊Subway directions:
Prince Street (N, R)
Broadway-Lafayette Street (B, D, F, M)
Spring Street (4, 6)

MiN Apothecary and Atelier opens a short list of the most popular cosmetics stores in the city. And not without reason.

The store is unique not only because of selling rare, hard-to-find, high-quality body products and toiletries, such as old-fashioned, handmade Plisson shaving brushes, but also because everything here is displayed in a nice, library-like setting.

The spacious interior contains broad windows, brick walls, partially covered with black, old-style wallpaper, solid dark-wood cabinets and shelves, heavy display tables, Chesterfield leather chairs and sofas, and a bar counter with stools.

To complete the picture, there are small pieces of antique furniture, handmade bird cages, a wooden toy horses, ceramic pots, live plants, brass and glass candlesticks and countless rows of apothecary jars of all sizes filled with mysterious potions and lotions arranged all around the store. All that plus a big magnifying glass next to an antique medicine bottle on the display table make this unusual place less a store and more an atelier of cosmetic art.

Converse Store

560 Broadway (at Prince Street)
www.converse.com
🚊Subway directions:
Prince Street (N, R)

The famous American flag by Jasper Jones is in MoMa. However, there are many other places in Manhattan where you can spot all sorts of American flags—painted and printed, big and small, common and rare, disposable and collectible, and just waving ones. Among all of them, there is also an American flag made from shoes. In fact, not made but arranged. And not just from any shoes but the shoes.

This one is on display in an industrial building, typical for this part of the city, a cast-and-iron historic district, with a cement floor and raw-brick walls covered with symbolic and iconic memorabilia and oversized black and white photos of rock'n'roll and basketball stars.

The place was converted into the Converse flagship store, acclaimed to be the largest of this kind throughout the world, and, to prove so, it carries every color and line of legendary shoes ever released. But just in case if something is not in stock, any requested model with a chosen pattern, soles and laces can be assembled at the custom-design counter at the back of the store. CS offers not only the most fashionable and unique sneakers for the majority of Converse lovers but also does its best to keep up with the needs of "minorities," because the Flag obliges to promote democracy even in a shoe store.

Prada

575 Broadway (at Prince Street)
www.prada.com
🚇Subway directions:
Prince Street (N, R, W)

As is said, fashion is the leading art of our century. If so, Prada in SoHo is a sort of fashionistas' MoMA, or at least the Gagosian Gallery—undoubtedly, a cult place for local dressy women.

It was created by one of the most prominent Dutch architects, Rem Koolhaas, for about "only" two thousand dollars per one square foot.

It is not a bargain; however, this expenditure seems to be worth every penny spent for creating this incredible place.

The central "point of interest" is paved with zebrawood "tsunami wave" starting from the first floor and descending to the basement level, used as the display space and—occasionally—improvised catwalk amphitheater.

There are also other architectural attractions inside, such as glass elevators and fitting rooms downstairs, which are translucent, but turn opaque at a touch of a button. They also provide an electronically generated rear view, much more panoramic and detailed than the traditional one.

Even the first-floor back space, in comparison to the rest of the store seeming perfectly normal, offers more visual attractions. Metal, night-club-style cages hanging from the ceiling on solid chains displaying Prada "basics," including pricey bags and other items (starting at one thousand bucks apiece) seems to be a very good idea for a ritzy and glitzy boutique, by the way.

The whole décor just speaks for itself, defining the Prada identity and certifying the top quality of one of the most prestigious brands in world fashion industry. Not to mention that everything here is literally en vogue.

Housing Works Bookstore Café

126 Crosby Street (between Prince and Jersey Streets)
www.housingworksbookstore.org
🚊Subway directions:
Broadway-Lafayette Street (B, D, F)
Prince Street (N, R)
Bleecker Street (4, 6)

Guests visiting New York usually don't put used-book stores on their top of must-see attractions lists. However, a few exceptions apply, like Housing Works Bookstore Cafe. Besides, how many bookstores deserve their own Wikipedia entry?

This one is a New York-based non-profit organization helping

AIDS suffering homeless people. So every penny from the bookstore café and the next-door thrift shop (staffed mostly by volunteers) support the foundation established two decades ago.

However, charitable purposes are not the only reason to visit the bookstore. The very place is worth visiting because of its rich collection of high-quality books (roughly 50,000 titles of hard-to-find titles), both old and new, on any subject and in any genre. Sentimental fans of music with crackles can find here an extensive collection of vinyl records, too.

The spacious two-story establishment is perfectly typical for this "cast-iron" district of downtown Manhattan, with the ceiling supported by rows of columns, antiquated oaken floors, the mezzanine, running around the whole space, with the wooden spiral staircase, mahogany paneled walls, the café at the back of the store with round tables right by the bookshelves, and a mixture of scents of wax and freshly brewed coffee (what a unique extravaganza of aromas). So being here is like traveling through time to the epoch when nobody even imagined e-books. Needless to say, it is a great place to relax, meet friends, and of course, buy good literature and music. Also, they offer free Wi-Fi, by the way.

REI

303 Lafayette Street (between Houston and Jersey Streets, Nolita)
www.rei.com
🚇Subway directions:
Broadway-Lafayette Street (B, D, F, M)
Bleecker Street (4, 6)
Prince Street (N, R)

There are many good retail outlets in the city selling sports gear and outdoor equipment, but only REI operates in the iconic, 19th-century Puck Building, the previous headquarters the J. Ottman Lithographic Company and Puck Magazine.

The architecture of the building is conspicuous: brick walls, columns and original ceilings, thoroughly restored and incorporated into the store interior design, the wood from the former structure turned into counters, refurbished canopies, tables and signs, two authentic chandeliers, two flywheels of 14 feet in diameter from the building's original power plant, renovated and exposed in the store space as well as about 40 genuine lithograph printing stones (at least, a century-old), which were discovered during the building restoration.

So the REI flagship store came into existence as a kind of museum, and it's a great idea because the place is worth visiting not only to buy a pair of trekking boots or a tent, but also to admire the mind-boggling architecture of the place.

The so-called Outdoor School (outdoor activities, camping and hiking instructions for beginners), and Outdoor Adventures (for more advanced adventurers) additionally make the place more appealing . And, by the way, it's still a great place to shop for any imaginable piece of sports equipment, no matter whether you are a mountain climber, a wilderness wanderer, or a participant of classes on survival in urban jungle.

Paper Source

83 Spring Street (between Crosby Street and Broadway)
www.paper-source.com
🚊Subway Directions:
Spring Street (4, 6)
Prince Street (N, R)
Broadway-Lafayette Street (B, D, F, M)

Isn't it a little freakish that, when it comes to stationery goods, Paper Source in SoHo (which found its way to the top of the best Manhattan paper vendors short list in just a few years), is a chain store first established in Chicago? It probably is, but the place really deserves its good reputation.

There are two other stores under that name, operating in New York—the one in Brooklyn and the other in Midtown West. All of them offer an incredibly wide selection of stationery and paper everything, from basic office supplies to rare, artsy stationery creations. The interior is typical for this part of the city—raw red-brick walls and industrial lighting.

In all its corners, there is an endless inventory of stationery goods from envelopes, boxes, wrappings, rolls of ribbons, cards, notepads and even scrapbooks to a large selection of unique paper gifts and craft kits, and New York theme paper keepsakes of all kinds.

However, there is something more that makes this place unique. After entering the store, you will see the catchy slogan of the Paper Source chain: "Everyday make something creative!" And they try to abide by that motto by offering paper-craft workshops regularly.

The place keeps the promise given by its name and is really "the source" of not only stationery but also of endless ideas about paper usage in all possible ways. Some of them are amazing, fun and truly inspiring. After visiting such a place, instead of keeping printing paper in a boring pile, it can occur to you to arrange it in a form of—let's say—The Empire State Building as this has happened to a local reporter lately.

Because creativity defines Manhattan itself, the store like this one is just condemned to succeed here.

Aedes Perfumery

(aka Aedes De Venustas)
7 Greenweech Avenue at Christopher Street
aka www.aedes.com
🚇Subway directions:
W4 Street (A, B, C, D, E, F, M)
Christopher Street-Sheridan Square (1, 2)
14th Street (1, 2, 3)

While a packaging is usually not the most important reason to visit a store, its black-and-gold boxes topped with fresh flowers obviously played a role in acclaiming this place as the best in the city, at least in beauty products category.

It is the first (and often the last) source of high-end perfumes and rare body products (usually impossible to find anywhere else) from all over the world. The perfumery—all purple and gold, furnished with heavy velvet curtains and carpeting, inlaid wood armoires with glass shelves, crystal chandeliers, cherry blossoms, and even a stuffed white peacock as well—not only looks like an old European art museum but also works as one. For example, the gem-cut flacon collection on display that contains antique rarities of fragrance history, including four-hundred-year-old Santa Maria Novella, original Aqua di Cologna and famous Aqua di Parma alike. As the name of the store translated from Latin means a Temple of Beauty, the place offers not only the perfume history lessons, but also provides around 40 best scents and bath and body cosmetic brands as well as a vast selection of home fragrances—room sprays, potpourri and candles. This red and gold enchanted beauty palace has something for everyone, and it's hidden somewhere in mysterious crystal flacons behind its rococo heavy velvet curtains.

C.O. Bigelow's Chemists
414 6th Avenue (at 9th Street)
www.cobigelow.com
🚇Subway directions:
W 4th Street (A, B, C, D, E, F, M)
6th Avenue (L)
Christopher Street-Sheridan Square (1, 2)

Sightseeing, particularly in Manhattan, is a painful and tiring experience, so it's good to know where to get some tourist-oriented remedies. Duane Reade pharmacies are almost at every corner so it is not a problem to buy headache pills and band-aids for sore feet. However, besides chain pharmacies, it is still possible to do it in a New Yorker's way as Mark Twain, Eleanor Roosevelt and Calvin Klein did. You can do it in C.O. Bigelow's Chemists, which opened just two doors from its today's location (then named Bigelow's Apothecaries) in 1836.

This historic place is not the oldest pharmacy in New York, it is the oldest drugstore in the United States. As a proof of this, in C.O. Bigelow's Chemists, there are rows of hundred-year-old apothecary jars, glass and delftware, hand-written prescriptions and formulas, and a ledger of 1905-1906 with names of the most prominent patrons of that period, including Mark Twain.

This pharmacy is not only the oldest but also one of the best in the city because of its famous home-brand homeopathic medicines and cosmetics. That is why, to relieve fatigue, headache, and sore feet, there is nothing better than the original C.O. Bigelow's Cold and Flu Herbal Soak Formula No. 122. and Lemon Body Cream—from New York, with love.

It is also the best source of rare, imported, exclusive and hard-to-find beauty products from Japan and Europe. The pharmacy is also the heaven of herbal remedies and cosmetics, all based on natural oils and extracts, and displayed in a spacious historic interior with the original, Victorian equipment under gas-lit chandeliers. No wonder it was the only place in Manhattan open during two East Coast blackouts, which makes it the most reliable pharmacy in New York.

EAST VILLAGE/LOWER EAST SIDE

The part of the city from Canal Street and east from Broadway near SoHo to Houston Street area is the city's most representative site of "ethnic" communities and the last place to shop in "the old New York style." Consequently, in this part of the city with its narrow, cobblestone streets and hundred-year-old townhouses, there are numerous little stores, delis and restaurants, resembling those in distant corners of the world. This is also an ideal location for visiting specialty shops (a great source of New York souvenirs) and bargain stores on Broadway near China Town, a few of blocks down and up Canal Street.

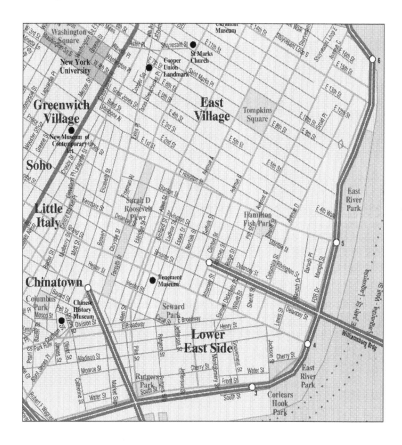

Not quite a naked skeleton – in a comfy hand-knit jersey at Kiehl's

Against Nature Atelier

159 Chrystie Street (between Delancy and Rivington Streets)
www.gainstnaturenyc.com
🚇Subway directions:
Bowery Street (J, M, Z)

Where should you go to find the best in New York men's custom-made and off-the-rack suits, jeans, shirts, and elegant accessories to complete the "circa 1880 western dandy appearance"? The right answer is—to a library! Not quite, of course, although Against Nature Atelier looks like an antiquated one, borrowing the interior design from the real place, which is rather unusual for a haberdashery store.

Even those upscale, like this one, offering ready-to-wear suits, elegant, finely crafted button-downs, premium, high-end custom-made jeans and unique silver and leather accessories. Surprisingly, other designers' boutiques in the best locations of the city do not coddle their particular clientele with this kind of shopping experience.

So even in Manhattan, it is not common to browse through high-quality merchandise alongside Chesterfield sofas, chrome lamps, leather-bound books, potted plants, terrariums, apothecary jars with mysterious content, vases of feathers, a baboon skull suspended in a glass dome, and a pair of stuffed albino peacocks—just to name a few.

All this is enough to recreate the refined atmosphere of fin-de-siècle Parisian high-society life.

Economy Candy Market

108 Rivington Street (between Ludlow and Essex Streets)
www.economycandy.com
🚇Subway directions:
Delancey Street (F)
Essex Street (J, M, Z)
2nd Avenue (F)

Economy Candy Market is definitely not a "secret" shopping destination because there is probably not a single city guide ever printed which does not include that specific store in its top ten list; and not without reason, this place is a real "candy store" for candy lovers of all generations.

A quaint tricycle, hanging from the ceiling with embossed brass panels is one of the first things attracting shoppers' attention after entering the store. It is a symbolic veihicle carrying them to "sweet lands" of their childhood.

The whole place, from floor to ceiling, is jam-packed with all imaginable and unimaginable kinds of candies ever made.

So, this is the only candy store in the city that offers everything—from old-fashioned button candies to jelly beans of any possible color and flavor, sold at the retro-style Jelly Beans Bar at the back of the store.

It is hard to believe, but Rowentree's fruit pastilles, Maynard's wine gums, gigantic pinwheel swirl lollipops, incredible choices of Paz dispensers, Jordan Almonds in every shade of pink (and in other colors too) are still available here. Apart from them, ECM offers the widest imaginable selection of jawbreakers and even almost forgotten Razzles, Cherleston Chews, and Zagnut bars are still available here as well as novelties and a vast assortment of chocolates and candies by the pound.

The old-time lollipops, jawbreakers and candy sticks are rarely present in popular candy stores throughout the city; that is why, the trip to Economy Candy Market is like a nostalgic travel to the happy days of childhood.

Patricia Field
306 Bowery (between Houston and Bleeker Streets)
www.patriciafield.com
Subway directions:
Bleeker Street (4, 6)
2nd Avenue (F)
Broadway-Lafayette Street (B, D, F, M)

Buying a spectacular boho skirt as a New York souvenir inspired by "Sex and the City" can be pricey, and buying it in the bedroom of the person who has defined a "New York style" herself seems to be just priceless.

However, it can happen thanks to the legendary designer and stylist, Patricia Field, who dressed Carrie Bradshaw, Ugly Betty, Shopaholic Girl, among others. She has converted her old apartment at Bowery it into a two-story, some 4,000-square-foot signature store with a retail space and a hair salon on the first floor.

Patricia's former living room and studio are the main part of the boutique, but her private bed, desk or other pieces of furniture are not there, at least, in sight. What is obviously present in the entire store all the time is the designer's rebellious spirit of a breaker of fashion rules. This is enhanced by red-brick walls, illuminated signs, mannequins wearing sex-shop style clothes and accessories, and peculiar pop-art details. All of these make this place fun and create an artsy atmosphere.

Patricia Field's presence manifests itself mostly in her printed patent leopard leather items, creations of pink sequin and feathers and unique accessories, guaranteed to be one hundred percent in New York style, which even Carrie Bradshaw would love.

John Varvatos

315 Bowery Street (between 1st and 2nd Streets)
www.johnvarvatos.com
🚇Subway directions:
2nd Avenue (F)
Bleeker Street (4, 6)
Broadway-Lafayette Street (B, D, F, M)

This Bowery Street location is one of three stores of the former designer in Ralph Lauren's team, John Varvatos. Although it offers the same merchandise that the other two, such as a wide selection of his modernly cut suits, outstanding sportswear, rock-inspired jackets, dress-down knitted linen skirts and one-of-a-kind artsy T-shirts, John Varvatos at 315 Bowery is just something much more than a retail store.

It was established at the location previously occupied by CGBG, an iconic, legendary music club founded in 1973, and originally intended to feature three musical styles—blues, bluegrass, and country.

The store owner decided to keep up with that glorious past of the place; that's why, inside you still may find dog-eared, partly tattered yellowed rock posters (all framed and glassed), band fliers dating back a half century, performance photographs, and even original makeshift wallpapers and graffiti.

The store décor consists mostly of rock memorabilia, among them there are vinyl records, antique radio equipment, and several vintage guitars that are kept in showcases throughout the store space or piled-up on the small stage as if being ready for the next generation of performers. The piano here serves a double purpose—the obvious one and as a display place. However, the most prominent feature of the store that attracts shoppers' attention is a floor-to-ceiling contemporary "art installation" compiled from old-time loudspeakers.

The effort to preserve the original interior of the music club, and to satisfy all those waxing nostalgic about that bygone era was undertaken—as John Varvatos once said, "to retain the part of the history, so that everybody can walk in off the street and experience a part of what was there."

As proof of visiting the place, you can buy one of JV-famous and pricey T-shirts.

Billy Reid

54 Bond Street (between Bowery and Lafayette Streets)
www.billyreid.com
🚇Subway directions:
Bleeker Street (4, 6)
Broadway-Lafayette Street (B, D, F, M)
2nd Avenue (F)

In New York, there are stores in former residential mansions and brownstones, industrial and dockyard buildings and even churches abandoned by their congregations, so, why not establish a store in a defunct theater?

Billy Reid occupied the New York City landmark building after Bouwerie Lane Theatre had been closed, and now it has its seat the Bowery street front.

To keep up with the place spirit, the store interior was decorated with the effort of recreating the appearance and atmosphere of the past, through vintage furniture placed around the historic staircase, deer heads on the walls with antique ornate coverings and cut-glass, porcelain, vintage photographs and bric-a-brac flea-market-style decorations, a couch made of old church pews, vintage apothecary cabinets, potted flowers and chandeliers.

All these items highlight the traditional quality and style of Billy Reid clothing and accessories, blazers with elbow patches, plaid button-downs and "perfect parlor dresses," since the store offers not only men's everything, from classic suits to Italian leather handmade shoes, but also the CDFA (the prestigious award bestowed by Council of Fashion Designers of America) winning designer's limited line of jeans and an entire women's collection as well. Including Apron Wiggle Dress (in the post-feminist world an apron is, of course, removable).

The visit to the store is like a time travel from which you can bring something nice and new, for example, a pair of limited-edition jeans.

Bond No. 9

9 Bond Street (between Lafayette Street and Shinbone Aly)
www.bondno9.com
🚊Subway directions:
Bleeker Street (4, 6)
Broadway-Lafayette Street (B, D, F, M)
Prince Street (N, R)

After a couple of hours in Manhattan, it may be hard not to agree that New York City smells like a cup of fresh-brewed Java coffee (milk, no sugar) with a citrus-floral spice with the blend of bergamot, lily of the valley plus pepper. All this thanks to the most competent fragrance hunters in NYC, working on defining, collecting and preserving the scents of the city's streets and neighborhoods (however, bear in mind that a short subway ride is not the best possible way to experience this aromatic sensation).

The result from that effort, trapped in the black bottle and named after a famous city logo "I Love New York," sells in in multiple locations of Bond No. 9 perfume chain stores throughout the city, so everybody can recollect the unique scent of Manhattan just by opening a star-shaped container at any time and place in the world.

The 33 other bottles contain the scents of various popular city's locations—from Central Park West to Coney Island in Brooklyn.

The collection of all the city's fragrances you can also buy in the Bond No. 9 flagship store, established in a historic townhouse on picturesque cobble-stoned Bond Street. The address number? Obviously, 9!

The store occupies the entire floor of the building, housing not only the retail space, arranged like a beauty parlor with oval mirrors along the walls, pastel counters and display tables, surrealistic, wavy, oneiric fresco on the ceiling and Dali-style mannequin-shaped stands as dram units as well as a "scent library" and a tea room. The store has a custom-blend fragrance station, giving customers a rare opportunity to create a unique, personal version of their own "New York signature scent" by themselves.

Besides the signature collection, the store with a historic city subway token as its logo on the display window, offers a rich assortment of fragrance products—body lotions, soaps and candles, including Wall Street scent candles to inspire all the aspiring Forbes-list conquerors.

Enchantments

424E. 9th Street (between 1st and A Avenues)
www.enchantmentsincnyc.com
🚇Subway directions:
1st Avenue (L)
3rd Avenue (L)
Astor Place (4, 6)

In New York, there is a store offering almost everything a witch or a wannabe witch and all kinds of sorcerers may need. Enchantments is its name, and it is fully justified. To complete the picture, not only does it sell occult stuff but also it is the center for learning the arcana of spells and black magic.

At the entrance, it appears quite conventional (the small skull in the corner...), but it is far more "enchanted" inside filled with different wizardry props and objects. Among them there are long rows of wooden cabinets containing magical herb jars, a gang of cats (black, of course) wandering randomly between shelves, crystal balls to look into the future, piles of brooms (presumably flying) in every corner and tons of candles literally everywhere.

If somebody needs, for instance, a solid cauldron to brew a magical potion, an incense stick to remove a hex or to cast a spell, or a celestial calendar to foretell the weather for tomorrow, will find all that stuff there. And if a customer wants to do all the mentioned above, but has no idea what to start with, there are "how to" books at hand.

In the rear counter, at the in-store carving post, custom-made candle carving is available while waiting, which is very convenient for every witchcraft novice because every such a candle is delivered with the detailed, spell by spell instruction.

The most desirable candles are these for new love, but there is one for everything here, from putting a hex on a disrespectful boss to winning a fortune, and, of course, returning soon to New York.

The store must have some enchanting powers by itself,

because most of the people who visit the place once, usually find a way to return here, sooner or later.

Halloween Adventure

104 4th Avenue (between 11th Street and 12th Street)
www.newyorkcostumes.com
🚇Subway directions:
Astor Place (4, 6)
14th Street-Union Square (4, 5, 6, Q, N, R)
3rd Avenue (L)

In the city with The "Vampire" State Building in the core of Downtown, Halloween goes on all year round. And so does the biggest and the most popular among costume stores in Manhattan— Halloween Adventure.

This two-story, 15 000-square-foot establishment tries to keep the promise not only in its "Halloween" part of the name but also in the "adventure" part, so the place looks like those historic sites and theme parks with staff dressed up as Rag Dolls and Jacques The Skeletons, and the like. The interior, full of the old posters, theatrical accessories and props, hosting even a little costume museum, make the decor like a setting from "Tales from the Crypt."

The decoration and costumes changes consecutively with the oncoming holydays, from Christmas to Valentines, Purim, Easter and so on.

However, not only Easter Bunnies and Love Birds define the store subsequence theme shows.

Even more important than holiday calendars are the heroes of the current popular movies, such as *Batman, Spiderman* or *Transformers*, and immortal characters from century-old fairytales and well-liked culture idols. So, in the store departments, arranged as huge walk-in-closets, there is something for Cinderellas, Aliens, Toy Soldiers, Xenomorphs, and Jimmys Hendrixes, of course, Elvis the Everlasting inclusive.

The significant part of the HA assortment comes from the theatre costume storage, so wannabe Carmens, or Madames Butterfly are not without their chances, either.

With the inventory of hundreds of props, hats, gloves, boots, fans, and, of course, masks of all kinds, the complete makeover is possible here in a mere one hour.

Kiehl's
109 3rd Avenue (between 13th and 14th Streets)
www.kiehls.com
🚇Subway directions:
3rd Avenue (L)
14th Street-Union Square (4, 5, 6, Q, N, R)

Googling Kiehl's, almost every link mentions the year of the pharmacy's establishment—that is 1851. In Europe, everything created about that date is just 165 years young.

Here, in New York, such age means something nearly prehistoric.

That is why, just by surviving so long, Kiehl's has earned the status of a city landmark. Frankly, in this case, there are more reasons for being considered number one.

One of them is pear tree. It might sound funny, but it is a historical fact that when the store opened in its original location at the corner of Third Avenue and 13th Street, a 200-year-old pear tree from the private orchard of the first New York governor, Peter Stuyvesant, still stood there as a famous local landmark. Thus, the pharmacy marks the very core of New York City's "antiquity."

Shortly after opening, the store built its reputation on a special line of homeopathic skin care cosmetics and high quality fragrant oils acclaimed to have extraordinary properties; you can discover them just reading their names, such as "Love Oil," "Money Drawing Oil," and the likes.

Oils have been Kiehl's specialty since 1920, when the forgotten sample of Original Musk Oil was discovered in the pharmacy's basement laboratory and—after its debut on the market in 1963, it became the most popular and most widely imitated fragrance in the world.

That "discovery" was possible, because all the mixtures, extracts and essences are "home-made" and prepared in the store previously situated just one door from its today's location, in a small three-story townhouse.

Almost all of the beakers, funnels, retorts, scales, hand written formulas and apothecary jars filling the antique wooden showcases in the Kiehl's interior are genuine and mostly come from the laboratory in the basement.

Also, the stores' furniture, crystal chandeliers and twentieth-century photographs are at least five decades' old. What age are the numerous skeletons glowering at the public from almost every corner of the store—it's hard to tell, but they also must be antique.

Even the beauty products, scent essences. And particularly the body line are based on traditional, Khiel's pharmacists' originated formulas, which made them a cult brand among ecology oriented Hollywood stars and New York celebrities.

All those old and famous assortments of Kiehl's products are available in the store, including original scents, black narcissus, cucumber and pear among others.

To save the shoppers' time for sightseeing, the lotions, oils and fragrances are nicely and conveniently packed in elegant sets (full descriptions inside) as a ready-made precious New York souvenirs.

Obscura Antiques & Oddities

207 Avenue A (between 12th and 13th Streets)
www. obscuraantiques.com
🚊Subway directions:
1st Avenue (L)
3rd Avenue (L)

Evan Michelson, one of the co-owners of Obscura Antiques & Oddities, once said, "We specialize in scientific antiques, medical antiques, taxidermy. A friend of mine called it, 'Stuff you didn't think you needed until you saw it. I call it, 'An alternative kind of beauty.'" This is the one and only New York place where you can see (and even buy) a mummy's head, a Tibetan skull (a genuine one), Victorian mourning pieces, vintage photos from funeral homes, a real casket, and the hundred-year-old medical book about hemorrhoid remedies and treatments.

This establishment, with its 275 square feet, still seems relatively small as being packed with thousands of incredible objects, leaving customers no more than, maybe, one-third of the space for shoppers.

The store is often compared to a walk-in-closet, stuffed with taxidermy animals, strange-looking creatures (preserved in formalin), suspicious, bygone-era poisons and mysterious ingredients in apothecary jars, skeletons and medical displays from the 19th century and even antique dental tools along with a set of very old dilators (still in working condition!). Just an oddity heaven full of stuff most people have never seen before, only a few steps away from the very busy Union Square.

The store is worth a visit for itself as a tourist attraction because of its floor to ceiling packed, hard to navigate interior. It is almost as famous as the Ripley's Believe It or Not Museum while not really being a museum itself, since it has become popularized by several television shows (especially, "Oddities" on the Science Channel) and multiple lifestyle magazines.

Even the name of the store "Obscura," the Latin "obscure," speaks for itself, promising a dark atmosphere and a taste of the thrill straight from Victorian vampire stories. The store, despite being painted all white and far less packed now, still representing "the other kind of beauty," and keeps this promise very well.

Antiques, curios, treasures, and more in Obscura Antiques and Oddities

CHELSEA AND UNION SQUARE

The former Lady's Mile, 6th Avenue from 14th to twenty something street, was successfully transformed into the area of affordable superstores: Bed, Bath&Beyond, TJ Maxx, Marshalls, to name a few. Also, 14th Street, from Union Square to the Chelsea Piers is one the most popular destinations for the best bargain fashion pieces in the city. The closer to the Piers, stores seem to be more upscale and sophisticated, including Chelsea Market, which was impressively renovated recently, Jeffrey's iconic "bargain for millionaires.". The Union Square area of 14th Street is considered as the "bargain district" extension, with Strand Bookstore, the Burlington Coat Factory department store (with the entire floor of DWS affordable shoes), Nordstrom Rack Basement and Best Buy.

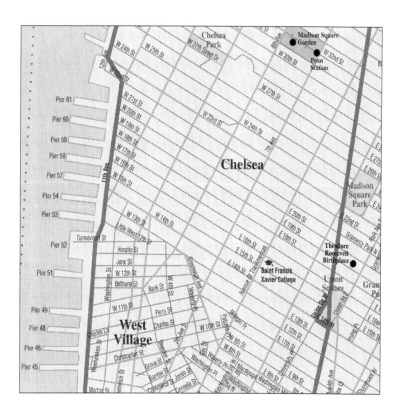

A spoony dress of spoons — only at Fishs Eddy

Chelsea Market

75 9th Avenue (between 15th and 16th Streets)
www.chelseamarket.com
🚇Subway directions:
14th Street (A, C, E)
8th Avenue (L)
18th Street (1, 2)

Though this is not the only place in New York where the city's history meets retail business, Chelsea Market is one of the most spectacular ones. Although this gigantic mall hosts mostly gourmet specialty stores (bread bakery, dairy bar, fish and seafood market, wine cellar, nuts and spices market, food court, etc.), you can buy here also clothing, home and kitchen appliances, and sundry souvenirs.

Chelsea Market in its previous life was the factory and head-quarters of the baking company New York Biscuit Co., which in 1898 merged with National Biscuit Company, known as NABISCO.

The factory, previously operated in this complex of red-brick buildings, occupied the entire block between 9th and 10th avenues at Chelsea. It was built between 1890 and 1930, and it became famous as the birthplace of one of the most recognized American pastry in the world—Oreo Cookie, which was originally baked here in 1912.

So the first thing that attracts attention after you enter the long concourse of red bricks and rusted steel is a "hall of fame"—hundred-year-old photographs, historical billboards, original last-century wrappers and packages, and press ads reminding the noble past of the place.

The renovation in 1998 by Vandeberg Architects preserved the history of Nabisco landmark, not only through documentary photos but, first of all, through keeping the structure of the building almost intact, and displaying all the remnants from its previous century in its interior. Thanks to the renovation, we can admire the original flooring (enhanced with light planks), rebar handrails and recycled industrial objects, from rusted pipes to gear-wheels, spread throughout the entire market space. Even a unique fountain is made from "rusty and broken" pipe and discarded drill bits. Similar, "affected" pipes are used in other decorative arrangements.

This industrial atmosphere is enhanced by stone seats, sculpted furnishings, dim artificial lighting and industrial props placed throughout the entire space.

Even some of retailers operating inside remind about the past of this place as a big baking factory, prepare their aromatic breads and any other imaginable pastries in full view of customers.

It is not surprising that Chelsea Market quickly and deservedly became one of the best shopping destinations in New York.

Carlos Miele

408 W 14th Street (between 9th and 10th Avenues)
www.carlosmiele.com
🚊Subway directions:
8th Avenue (L)
14th Street (A, C, E, 1, 2, 3)

How may a flagship store of a famous designer, performer and creator of museum art installations look like? Probably, the best answer is—the New York salon of the Brazilian-origin fashion world icon, Carlos Miele.

His Manhattan store is a materialization of his artistic credo: "a new dialogue between two worlds that wouldn't originally meet, but can and must coexist (...) special beauty of natural landscapes biodiversity and exuberance of popular culture."

So, on the one hand, the place resembles an all-white, alien spacecraft, and on the other hand—a gigantic organic cell. Every line in this immaculate interior seems to be opposite to any geometrical regularity.

The architect responsible for the project, Hani Rashid, filled the store's space with sculpture-like, Noguchi and Moore inspired forms, which dissolve the natural boundaries among the floor, the ceiling and the walls, creating streamlined, self-contained, enclosed spaces used as displays, but also as rest areas, placed throughout the entire store.

Despite all those architectural details, the interior looks definitely unreal.

That impression is even stronger because the mannequins that present the last Carlos Miele collection seem to levitate inside white "cells" as if they were well-dressed passengers from a Fashion Planet spacecraft, visiting the place to start a new breed of fashionistas in the heart of Manhattan.

Strand Bookstore
828 Broadway (between 12th and 13th Streets)
www.strandbooks.com
🚇Subway directions:
Union Square-14th Street (L, N, Q, R)
Union Square-14th Street (4, 5, 6)

If any of Manhattan's bookstores deserves the status of the city's landmark, undoubtedly, Strand Bookstore does. Its iconic red and white logo has been very well known to New York's most devoted bookworms for almost 80 years.

It is a mecca for readers where they can find about 2.5 million mostly used books (a road paved with them would be 18 miles long) of all genres, on any subject, the latest editions and those out of print, rare, collectible, old and new, in a nutshell, just almost any book you cannot find anywhere else in NYC.

The store occupies a huge space on four floors in a corner building on Broadway, remembering its industrial past, so it looks a little "old and dirty" as all the buildings in the neighborhood. When you enter the store, you will instantly catch the (pleasant) scent of books, and see the "signature chaos" all over the store; however, don't be deceived by appearances, every book here has its precise location on the shelf in accordance with the catalog.

So browsing through the countless, floor-to-ceiling

shelves in the narrow dark aisles seems to be an amazing experience of feeling lost as if you were in a maze. If you cannot find the book you are searching for on one of the floors, you may try it in the basement that looks like a dust-covered dungeon; who knows, maybe you will come across a treasure trove—a very rare book whose existence has never occurred to you, even in your boldest dreams.

Urban Outfitters
526 6th Avenue (at 14th Street)
www.urbanoutfitters.com
🚊Subway directions:
6th Avenue (L)
14th Street (F, M)
14th Street (1, 2, 3)

Being one of Manhattan's most popular locations representing an acclaimed teenage urban style, Urban Outfitters in Greenwich Village usually measures up to the highest expectations by offering the latest lines of products—from clothing to home accessories, gifts, electronic gadgets and even rare books.

The brand identity also fulfills the expectations thanks to the store's split-level interior décor arranged according to "urban" New York style, which, as it is believed here, can be fully appreciated and admired only by a true New Yorker.

For the rest of customers, it may be a little tough to enthuse about cracked, concrete floors, raw, partially painted white red-brick walls, tarnished metal fixtures, iron pillars, "technical" lightning and other architectural details testifying to the industrial past of this retail space.

However, in Manhattan, a store or home interior made from city detritus—broken window frames and door panels, rusty bath and kitchen fittings, antique vent grates, verdigrised door knobs—all constitute a "signature look" expressing very New Yorkish taste.

And Urban Outfitters seems to be one of the best places in the city where true New Yorkers can satisfy their nonconformist attitude to their "signature habitat."

Barnes & Noble Bookstore
33E at 17th Street-Union Square
www.bn.com
🚇Subway directions:
14th Street-Union Square (N, Q, R)
14th Street-Union Square (4, 5, 6)
14th Street-Union Square (L)

Megastores are more retailtaining than smaller ones simply by definition. Wider space equals richer inventory, and richer inventory equals more to choose from or just browse. But even if the Barnes & Noble Bookstore on Union Square is one of the less boring places to buy books and press in the city just by the above-mentioned definition, the place invites customers not only to its many book departments but also to different events, such as lectures, book signings, and concerts.

It is worth mentioning that the building of this B&N location has a very rich history. The first New York bookstore under that name in Midwest opened in 1917 at 5th Avenue and 18th Street, near the place where the other B&N store still exists.

The establishment on Union Square opened in a former home of the legendary Century Publishing Company in a landmark building with a brick, terra-cotta and stone masonry façade and a mansard roof. Its mahogany stairway and inner doors with massive two-way brass hinges, the tile floor of the lobby and other historic, old-looking interior with architectural details evoke the days of Mark Twain, whose novels were published here.

In such surroundings even the mass-retail bookseller's chain store looks far nobler than usually, not only by its Noble name itself.

Taking into account the chain prices, roughly one-third lower than everywhere else, the widest imaginable book selection as well as movies, creative gifts and paraphernalia on the first floor and all children's stuff from literature to games, toys and Lego parlor on the second floor, a visit here guarantees a real retailtainment experience. What's more, the store also houses public toilets (not so obvious in Manhattan), and a Starbuck's café inside, for those wanting to read books more clearly after a cup of good coffee.

ABC Carpet and Home

888 Broadway (between 18th and 19th Streets)
www.abccarpet.com
🚆Subway directions:
14th Street-Union Square (N, Q, R)
23rd Street (4, 6, N, R)

The history of the city is abundant in true stories about New Yorkers' careers in the American way—from rags to riches. And here is one of them.

Long time ago, a poor newcomer from Austria, Sam Weinrib, earned his living selling used carpeting and linoleum from a pushcart in the Lower East Side area. His son, who took over the family business, expanded it by renting a small store in the neighborhood. The grandson of the company's founder moved the store to a bigger space in a better location. In the conclusion of this story, almost a century later, his great grandson with the family bought and renovated the six-story Sloane Building, the place that used to be the finest rug and upholstery store in the entire city. Since then, that is—1980, it still has been the best New York establishment in this branch, belonging to the Weinribs, the family descendants who truly deserve the ownership of their "ABC Carpet and Home."

The multilevel store in former Sloan Building is still worth its reputation of being the first New Yorker's choice when it comes to home decoration.

ABC Carpet and Home has it all: Swedish beds, silk duvet covers, cashmere blankets, antique sideboards, hand-blown Venetian chandeliers, coffee-table-sized glass greenhouses for just one exotic plant to grow in artificial light, Tiffany-style lamps, ceramic mugs filled with silk orchids, modern mosaic tables, and French copper cookware. All of these items are displayed on the main floor, just at the entrance, and arranged as "The Parlor"—the store's own version of a gigantic movie setting, perfect for Tim Burton's next feature film about an eccentric upstate millionaire, or a promotion ad of the Hammond Castle Museum (Massachusetts).

However, this is only a small portion of ABC's inventory, which occupies the remaining floors, and it consists of fabric and trimmings, bed and bathroom items, kitchenware, pieces of art and antiques—just anything from quality aprons to zebra rugs.

As the outstanding lamp or rare rug may not be easy to pack into a small airplane suitcase as a New York souvenir, an original pillow, frame, artsy stationery or a pair of fine bookends seems to be quite acceptable. And the inside restaurant is rated as quite good, too.

Fishs Eddy

889 Broadway (between 19th and 20th Street)
www.fishseddy.com
🚇Subway directions:
23rd Street (N, R, 4, 6)
14th Street-Union Square (N, Q, R)

The authentic New York style kitchen is supposed to be modest, a little bit rustic, not too marbly nor dominated by modern appliances. In such a place, there should be and, in fact, there usually is some space for old-fashioned, fabric tablecloths, hand-painted cookie jars, stoneware flower pots with fresh basil growing on the windowsill, wicker baskets and a row of old dog-eared family cookbooks. In many Upper West Side apartments, half-century-old kitchen cabinets are usually not replaced with new ones. Upper-West-Siders just prefer antique kitchenware as do many other New Yorkers.

The best source of this kind of items is the store whose interior is arranged in the style similar to a typical (only bigger) New York kitchen, and here it is—Fishs Eddy.

The store with rustic wooden floors, well remembering the last century, is furnished with an old-style kitchen cupboard with threadbare surfaces and weather-beaten but still usable, wide tables, used as a display space for hundreds of cutlery (some even disposable), crockery, china, and glassware as well as wooden, linen and fabric items towering up in literally every smallest vacant space and corner.

This is the right address when it comes to replace a broken faience cup, to find the missing piece to a century-old table set, and to complement the still piling collection of table linen with new napkins and tablecloths. Also, it is a very good place to buy New York-style cooking manuals.

The store is conveniently located near the busy tourist destination—Union Squar; that is why, many of the above-mentioned items decorated with New York motifs and themes can be considered as souvenirs.

The only warning while browsing in these incredibly well-stocked china shop is not to behave like a bull because the store seems to be a little too small for all the inventory so creatively packed inside.

New Balance New York
150 5th Avenue (at 20th Street)
www.newbalance.com
🚇Subway directions:
23rd Street (N, R, F, M, 4, 6)

Ordering custom-made shoes usually means a long waiting time, and it is expensive; what's more, it is almost impossible to do because shoemakers are an endangered species. However, it doesn't apply to New York anymore, since the sneakers company from Boston opened its first "experience" store in Flatiron district. The associates from the company's factory in Maine can make a pair of customized sport shoes from the current New Balance collection while you wait, in about an hour, at the cost of less than one hundred dollars. The whole production process is easy to follow because the assembly showcase called "Demonstration Area" is conveniently located just at the entrance, behind the glass wall. So you can see the stitching mechanism and the rest of the machinery, even without entering the store, from the street through the display window.

The shoes, packed into the branded bag with the "Made in New York" label on it, could be tested on the spot, on the in store two-lane running track (a camera here can take pictures of the runner and, on demand, post them automatically on Facebook as the proof of your extra-sightseeing activities while in New York).

On the 4,000-square-foot floor, amidst restored original brick walls and floor-to-ceiling columns, there are even more historic stitching machines and objects of art that have witnessed the over one-century company's past. However, there is enough space for conventional racks, shelves, displays with shoes, sport clothes, and other accessories. You cannot miss the so called "heritage ribbon" hanging from the ceiling, displaying the company's history from the beginning through the present to the future—bright, of course.

The store is the proof that the owners have found a new balance between production and commerce...and enter-tainment, obviously.

Comme des Garçons

520 W 22nd Street (between 10th and 11th Avenues)
www.comme-des-garcons.com
🚊Subway directions:
23rd Street (A, C, E)
14th Street (A, C, E)

This French-sounding, Japanese imagination-inspired store offers wearable pieces of art. Comme des Garçons sells sculpture-like clothes deigned by Rei Kawakubo, the famous designer and founder of the store, and her colleague Junya Watanabe.

Comme des Garçons is French for "like boys," but despite a "boyish style," all the clothes are for young (or feeling young) gentlemen and ladies, too.

After entering the store through the entrance looking like an "organic," aluminum tunnel, everything here encourages to explore every bit of the place and promises a challenging adventure following the stereotype of "a boy's nature." The interior, designed by Takao Kawasaki, is characterized by white walls with bright-color accents and movable silvery screens, which allow the space to be rearranged very easily. That's why, the store may look different every time you visit it.

However, despite its architecture and décor, the most challenging items here are definitely the clothes themselves because trying on a CDG garment is like solving a puzzle consisting of three sleeves, five pockets (two of them on the back) and mysterious buttons hidden inside.

When eventually the "riddle" is solved, the jacket or skirt, or even a simple T-shirt—each of them turns into a matchless piece of wearable art.

City Quilter

133 W 25th Street (between 6th and 7th Avenues)
www.cityquilter.com
🚆Subway directions:
23rd Street (1, 6, C, E, F, R)

What could be the best souvenir from sunny and hot summer days of New York for long, freezing winter nights far away from Manhattan? Where to look for a gift which will be more useful and original than a plastic, Chinese-made green figurine of the Statue of Liberty, dozens of banal postcards, and all kind of knick-knack with "I ♥ NY" logo. Where to go for something very New Yorkish, from New York, and at the same time, intriguing and involving, and providing a unique experience?

In Manhattan, there are many really interesting shopping destinations, but those who search for a gift that requires some personal touch, City Quilter seems to be just the right place.

In our times almost nobody quilts, especially in New York. If somehow somebody still does, it's obviously done just for fun, like any artistic hobby, this time, with a traditional American background.

City Quilter, which being a regular fabric store, also provides sewing and quilting classes and holds its own theme "quilt art" gallery.

Established 50 years ago by a couple of artists, in a 4,000-square-foot Chelsea location, it offers more than 4,000 rolls of fabrics (mostly cotton), and specializes in all kinds of textiles as well as sewing and quilting accessories. They also carry books and magazines on the subject, and unique New York gifts made from the store's own line of fabrics inspired by New York iconography: landmarks and popular tourist destinations. So they have, for instance, warm and cozy "New York Day & Night" pillows, black and white quilts as well as quilted oven mitts with subway map prints, and, of course, a big selection of city-inspired fabrics line, including "Old New York," "NYC Subway", "Times Square," "New York Line by Line," and "Susy's New York" themes.

City Quilter also sells sewing kits, which enable even those who never held a needle in their hands to make a quilt or whatever—a tote bag or a towel with New York motifs, by themselves.

Everything needed for this kind of work is possible to buy here for just a couple of bucks.

The pleasure and satisfaction from making a cozy quilt with the Empire State Building, Brooklyn Bridge or Times Square with his or her own hands cannot be overrated.

The author is exploring the silky fabric of matter in City Quilter

MIDTOWN WEST

The part of the city from 30th Street and Herald Square to Times Square 59th Street and Columbus Circle is a historic commercial district with distinctive department stores, flagships of popular brands and specialty stores. About 30 blocks of Garment District and Theatre District serve as a kind of display windows full of the best everything New York can offer, especially its garment industry, including sample sales of the hottest and biggest names in fashion. Times Square and the Rockefeller Center area are occupied mostly by popular brands and specialty megastores, including Toys-"R"-Us and Disney's, Lego.

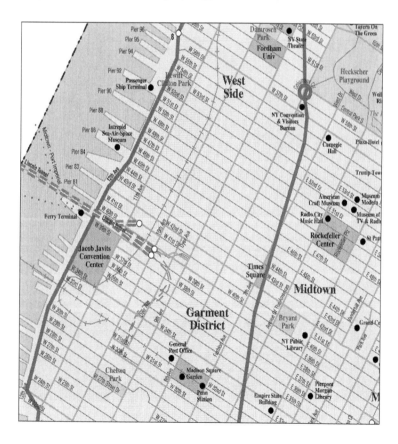

If I were a child, yubby dibby, dibby, dibby, dibby, dum...in Toys "R" Us

Fantasma Magic Shop

421 7th Avenue (at 34th Street)
2nd Floor
www.fantasmamagic.com
🚇Subway directions:
34th Street-Penn Station (1, 2, 3)
34th Street-Herald Square (B, D, F, M, N, Q, R)

The most famous magician, Harry Potter, is British; however, it is not London that seems to be the most magical city in the world but New York . There are many reasons for that, of course; one of the most obvious is Fantasma Magic Shop.

It is the only place of this kind in the city, but just this one stands for a dozen conventional shops of this specialty, stocked only with everything magic, such as wands, enchanted caps and manuals for conjuring tricks. In this store, literally nothing is ordinary.

Even walking into the store is unlike entering any other shop in the vicinity because it is well-hidden on the second floor of a plain-looking building. But the reward is worth the effort of squeezing through a narrow staircase to reach the destination. It is not just a store, it's also a magical club with a small scene and a red drop-curtain, where live magic shows are performed almost non-stop. Moreover, it is Sa museum, more specifically, a little museum of magic.

FMS's history corner is dedicated to the greatest magician of all time, Harry Houdini. The red fabric lined walls are covered with numerous old framed posters and press articles about him, and in the middle of the establishment, there is a small display with chains, lockers, cages and other antique props Houdini used in his incredible and hard to believe shows.

However, first of all, Fantasma Magic Shop, as its name suggests is a store. That is why, on the astonishingly plain-looking displays, there is literally everything an aspiring conjurer as well as a professional one may need. Lessons of

80

magic are also available on demand (free of charge if you buy something). It is also possible to buy a paid training session about how to perform a specific magic trick from those presented during the store's live shows.

So visiting Fantasma Magic Shop is not just a shopping trip for usual magical accessories, but it's also like attending an entertainment club and a museum at the same time. A one-of-a-kind magical experience of magic.

B&H Photo-Video
420 9th Avenue (between 33rd and 34th Streets)
www.bhphotovideo.com
🚇Subway directions:
34th Street-Penn Station (A, C, E, 1, 2, 3)
28th Street (1, 2)

B&H Photo-Video is the same kind of store like, say, Disney Store—every child wants to visit it.

In case of B&H, the only difference is that it's a place for inner children rather or for those just a little more grown up—big boys and big girls, bearing in mind that these days everybody wants the latest electronic gadgets and equipment.

Usually, the best stores in the city, including Adorama and Best Buy, offer the largest assortment of photo-video gear, computers and other high-tech stuff at discounted and competitive prices. However, only B&H Photo-Video gives its customers more.

Beyond anything else, the store's sales assistants are incredibly competent, patiently answering any question and offering the hands-on trying of everything in the store, despite the wild crowd surging around at any given time of day.

The selection of product seems to be unlimited. They have everything a customer could need, and they have it in stock (meaning—to buy it without weeks of waiting).

So they know everything and they have everything, especially when it comes to photo and video equipment.

Additionally, the store provides repair services, trade-on deals and used electronics accessories (even the smallest and rarest ones at very reasonable prices). B&H also offers free instructional classes every month.

Even if you are not going to buy anything in the store, it is still worth visiting it to see its world-famous microphone room. However, what is especially worth seeing is a unique conveyer system with its lifts, suspension rails and colorful containers, delivering every purchase to registers in no more than five minutes. This system is exceptional in the world, extremely efficient and, in a way, entertaining.

Without a shadow of a doubt, not only does B&H satisfy its customers, but it also pleases the shoppers' inner children.

Macy's

151 W 34th Street (between 7th Avenue and Broadway)
www.macys.com
🚇Subway directions:
34th Street-Penn Station (1, 2, 3)
34th Street-Herald Square (B, D, F, M, N, R, Q)
34th Street-Penn Station (A, C, E)

Is this million-square-foot commercial space enough to house the world's largest department store? Not necessarily, but New Yorkers believe so, pronouncing Macy's the biggest retailer worldwide.

It is also one of the oldest emporiums in the city (opened in 1858), and probably the only store under the sun that has its own annual parade—the Macy's Thanksgiving Parade, the sumptuous tradition that started in 1924.

Because of its history and architecture, it is undoubtedly a landmark, featuring original, previous century marbles, chandeliers, mirrors, carpets, and the oldest in the city, still working escalators as well.

One of the last old-time department stores still offers the wide variety of "everything you would need to furnish your home," as well as countless items of clothing, jewelry, accessories, cosmetics and lingerie—everything of all brands, from exclusive to popular ones.

Under a big red star—the store's logo, Macy's has the largest in the city, two-floor shoe department, a bridal suite with a walkway platform, burger bars, coffee nooks and the Cellar Bar & Grill, not to mention new amenities planned after 400-million-dollar renovation, which has already brought the Herald Square Café with exotic coffees, artisan chocolates and fine champagnes, and the Stella 34 Trattoria.

The store is still undergoing massive renovation (scheduled 2012-2015) transforming into one of the most technologically advanced, fashion-forward and exciting shopping destinations in the world, with new designer's departments, multi-level luxury shops, and other epicurean pleasures.

And, as all of us certainly know, thanks to the famous movie "Miracle of the 34th Street," the original winter Santa Claus' residency will remain intact at the Winter Wonderland on the eighth floor, waiting for all children, every year before Christmas.

H&M

1 Herald Center/Herald Square (between Broadway and 6th Ave.)
www.hm.com
🚇Subway directions:
34th Street-Herald Square (N, R, Q, B, D, F, M)

H&M, a Swedish global fast-fashion trendsetter opened its flagship in Manhattan in May 2015. It is currently this retail chain's biggest store in in the world, the 13th one in the city—exactly 13 years after the first H&M emporium opened on Herald Square, in one of the most prestigious and touristy locations in Manhattan, right in front of the famous Macy's department store (on the opposite page).

It offers a very wide assortment of the trendiest clothing, accessories, lingerie, footwear, and home décor at affordable prices.

The H&M flagship occupies the former location of one of New Yorkers' favorite chain Daffy's, which won their heart with the slogan "bargain for millionaires." So, probably, it is not a coincidence, and H&M wants to duplicate its predecessor's attitude success (of course, excluding the liquidation of Daffy's all 19 stores in 2014).

All the evidence points to success: 63,000 square feet on four floors (indeed impressive), 34 registers, two entrances, two elevators, a glass 53-foot façade with huge LCD screens showing H&M's latest collections, 30-foot-high atrium on the second level, and, of course, the brand itself.

The interior design is also spectacular with its numerous neons and mirrors surrounded by both glass walls and snow-white ones. All the space is brightly illuminated by hundreds (if not thousands) of nicely arranged "brightly shining balls." All this creates a sense of spatiality and neatness.

On the second floor, against the background of transparent glass wall, an authentic DJ provides music and, obviously, all those scratching and scrubbing sounds produced by his fingers and vinyl records on his mixing console.

It's noteworthy that the store has introduced many technological innovations to make shopping easier both for the sales assistants and shoppers by equipping its 40 fitting rooms with their own cash registers and heat sensors showing which room is occupied.

However, not this flagship's size and new technologies make it so attractive but rather its widest and most complete selection of merchandise of all H& stores in the world.

It's true that Macy's is the largest department store in the world (2.2 million square feet) and it's a living retail legend. but H&M's 63.000 are also impressive and leaves other fast-fashion retailers far behind.

Maybe this H&M's megastore will soon pass into legend, too. All the more so because John Legend himself, a famous American singer, has cut the ribbon.

Urban Outfitters (Flagship)

1333 Broadway
urbanoutfitters.com
🚊Subway directions:
34th Street-Herald Square (B, D, F, M, N, Q, R)

The Urban Outfitters brand originates from its first retail outlet in Pennsylvania, and now it has international status, consistently creates its image of a company that meets the needs of demanding young people from big cities. Of course, "youth" means "the young in spirit" at any age, who follow the style offered by UO—best defined by the words: modern, vanguard, metropolitan, natural, unforced, eco, vintage, hippyish, and, after all, free from any conventions.

In 2014 the new Urban Outfitters store opened in Manhattan, nearby the Biggest Department Store in the World, famous Macy's, between Herald Square and Broadway. Unlike the other stores of this brand in Manhattan (one of them in this guide on page 69), already very popular among the city's fashionistas, this one was acclaimed as a flagship, and it seems to be more like a department store than a regular retail outlet.

In fact, it is not the first UO of this kind in New York since the biggest establishment under this name operates in Williamsburg, Brooklyn, as the Nine 8 concept store. But the place opened at Herald Square is definitely the largest in Manhattan. Moreover, it is very versatile, hosting under its roof many other fashionable brands.

The entire interior is an open space for implementing the idea of "a store in a store." On three and a half levels, you can find something for yourself: a garment, a pair of shoes, hi-fi stereo system, CDs, interior design items, cosmetics, and many other typical OU's products.

However, as it hosts many other brands, you can buy here, for instance one or two of more than 1000 rare vinyl records at the Amoeba Music stand from California. By the way,

400 of those vinyl records are sold exclusively in this location.

Right next to beauty department operates a branch of Harroin Salon from Los Angeles, where you can restyle your hair into the most fashionable looks or buy hair accessories and cosmetics.

On the first floor, there is a large store with sportswear and sports equipment. If you need a caffeine boost, or you just like good coffee, you can stop by Intelligentsia Coffee bar from Chicago, where besides coffee, you can eat delicious desert or have a snack.

If you are an aspiring photographer or just a shutterbug, you should visit the photo department, and the Instagram Printing Station (the name speaks for itself).

There are also photo stations near fitting rooms on the second floor for aficionados of selfies, who can, trying on clothes and accessories, see for themselves their changed looks in the photos.

However, what is the most important here is this unique New York style, defined and popularized by Urban Outfitters stores.

It is distinguished by simplicity, or even austerity of brick walls, with patches of peeling-off paint, concrete floors and ceilings with visible, woodwork made of unseasoned timber, uncovered rusted pipes, factory-style lighting, etc. This all creates a visual code, which is very well-understood by Mnhattanites.

The store's collections, accessories also follow this visual code; that is why, they are usually made of natural, good-quality, but looking poor and worn-out fabrics, in washed-out grey colors with simple, delicate patterns or with no patterns at all. And, of course, in a simple cut.

So, if somebody wants to know what „New York style" really means, the best way to learn is just paying a visit to any of the Urban Outfitters stores—preferably, the flagship on Herald Square in Manhattan.

Victoria's Secret

1328 Broadway (between 34th and 35th Streets)
www.victoriasecret.com
🚇Subway directions:
34th Street-Herald Square (B, D, F, M, N, Q, R)
34th Street-Penn Station (1, 2, 3)
42nd Street-Bryant Park (B, D, F, M)

Though New York is not the city of angels as Los Angeles is, some angels settled here for good. And though they are not so numerous, they grace the city's landscape with their presence, being chosen from the most beautiful angels in the entire heaven by Victoria's Secret, the world-famous chic woman's lingerie store. They are top lingerie models, so it's not surprisiing, dressed only in pieces of classy underwear. As they barely dressed, one might suspect that they come from "fallen angels." Anyway, they are beautiful, and spreading their wings, they efficiently advertise silky merchandise of the store.

After a few years of the angels' presence in display windows, gigantic billboards, and local TV shows, the business expanded, and the city desperately needed more heavenly staff. So the angels' celestial beauty covered only with wings (of course, besides the lingerie, including all-kind hosiery, panties, bras sports underwear, "special event" lace and feather corsets, silk night gowns, etc.) also helped to promote the brand accessories and fragrances—everything packed in distinctive pink-striped shopping bags with silver yarn handles. In the store there are wingless angels as well, who work at the back of the store, in the fitting rooms area, helping shoppers to choose the right-sized bra or other piece of "unmentionables." They also advise them on the best gift for that special someone. It is much to choose from, bearing in mind all the plethora of undies in this three-story lingerie emporium.

Following the last renovation, the New York angels' official residence on Herald Square acquired not only thousands of additional square feet but also the full-sized catwalk, which may attract even more angels, and this in turn can attract more shoppers to Herald Square. The Victoria Secret flagship store expansion proved that to make its brand cult and famous, there is no better way than a heavenly intervention.

This is the only place in New York (or even in the world) where you can see an angel wearing a bikini.

Toys "R" Us Times Square

1530 Broadway (at 45th Street)
www.tousrus.com
🚇Subway directions:
Times Square-42nd Street (S, 1, 2, 3, 7)
49th Street (N, Q, R)

In New York everything is by definition the largest in the world. This obvious truth applies not only to skyscrapers, banks, corporations...and potholes in the streets but also stores.

And without a shadow of a doubt, in this case, bigger is better.

For instance, in a smaller space it wouldn't be possible to install a full-size (60 feet) working Ferris wheel inside. Under the same roof, there is enough room for a private "Jurassic Park" with a five-ton and 34-foot tall life-size animatronic T-Rex dinosaur (in action, whatever that means). It looks almost the same as the critter in the Museum of Natural History nearby—only better because of its more naturalistic appearance and thrilling roar. It's easy to guess that all children, regardless of age, prefer this one in Toys "R" Us...

In case you or your kids have not yet seen the major landmarks of NYC, you can do it here. In one place you can sightsee Manhattan Island, the Empire State Building, and The Statue of Liberty—all made from Lego blocks. Of course, they are much smaller, but owing to that fact, it is more convenient to explore them. As the old proverb says, "You can't have your cake and eat it too (or have the best of both worlds).

In contradiction with that downsizing is a Barbie dollhouse here. It is much bigger than the original and looks like a "real" two-story building (a little too pink inside, for my taste). Of course, such a megastore for children absolutely must hast have a candy department, and it has one, with a Willi Wonka's-like sweets factory in the back of the store.

In this 11,000-square-foot space, packed with myriads of toys in all possible sizes, colors, designs, complexity, price, immovable or animated, silent, buzzing, squeaking, or talking, and more, there is a favorite spot for everybody regardless of age and gender. However, children, by definition, have the highest priority here.

Forever 21

1540 Broadway (between 45th Street and 7th Avenue)
www.forever21.com
🚇Subway directions:
49th Street (N, Q, R)
Times Square -42nd Street (S)
47th-50th Streets/Rockefeller Center (B, D, F, M)

Who doesn't want to be kissed by a beautiful model? And to be put into her shopping bag forever? These things are only possible in Forever. To be more specific, in Forever 21, and only in one location of this "fast fashion" popular chain—on Times Square.

The 90,000-square-foot retail mammoth is acclaimed to be the biggest flagship of Forever 21 in Manhattan, but not only the size makes it jaw-dropping.

This "eye-popping factor" results from futuristic, all-white interior design with some astonishing features and, above all else, wide and varied merchandise selection. Forever 21's four floors are full of affordable trendy clothes and accessories for literally everybody—from fussy teenagers to local hard-to-please fashionistas from Greenwich Village and Soho.

"Fast fashion" is just like "fast everything" else, so, for Forever 21 all the customers are equally entitled to affordable but fashionable and good quality clothes. Forever 21 is, with all respect, not Bergdorf and Goodman, which does not mean that some of the garments from F21 can't survive till the next season or two. The strongest magnet to the store is, obviously, fashion. Miles and tons of fashion everything, and...even more fashion to "shop till you drop" for about 100 dollars.

However, its 150 fitting rooms, spatial interior with futuristic design, and numerous props make a visit here even more as if staying in a fashion addicts' heaven, housing an upscale "tree home" in the men's department and the original yellow cab on the lowest floor, not to mention LED screens everywhere.

A ginormous spy tech-powered billboard on the façade beats all the other screens hands down. It interacts with a crowd on Time Square through an equally gigantic beautiful model. She seems to pick a person out of the crowd and kiss the lucky one. The kiss is like a spell turning such a person into a fashion lover forever or, at least, a forever fan of Forever 21.

Disney Store

1540 Broadway (at 46th Street)
www.disneystore.com
🚇Subway directions:
49th Street (N, Q, R)
Times Square-42nd Street (S)
47th-50th Streets-Rockefeller Center (B, D, F, M)

This Disney Store has it all: a merry-go-round by the entrance (but only for teddy bears and dolls), a twenty-foot pink and golden castle, an "enchanted" forest of white trees, a row of singing Ariel dolls and even Ridemakerz to make customized toy cars. And, of course, the Magic Mirror where, after waving a magic wand, an animated Princess appears.

It is no overstatement to say that there are myriad Disney toys everywhere.

Obviously, housing so many objects for all-age-group children to play doesn't leave much space for the shoppers, despite the store's 20,000 square feet on its two floors.

All in all, every store would be probably too small for all the seekers after their halcyon days of childhood, so no wonder the Disney temple on Times Square is always crowded. However, it seems not to be an unfair price for this one-of-a-kind travel through time experience. Of course, actual children love the place, too.

After full-scale renovation, this particular store is more "New Yorky" than ever because of its murals with iconic Disney characters, for instance, Miki Mouse running through Manhattan, a Mickey Mouse Statue of Liberty, and the like. And, of course, the store carries "Mickey Mouse New York" T-shirts, too.

However, it's not only about the magic of New York City but mostly about the Disney world of magic, exactly as the "World Largest Disney Store" should be.

Hershey's Times Square

48th Street and Broadway (between 48th and 49th Streets)
www.hersheysstore.com
🚊Subway directions:
49th Street (N, Q, R)
50th Street (1, 2, A, C, E)

Switzerland has its world-famous Milka and Lindt chocolates, England—Cadburry; and what these brands made for their countries of origin, Hershey's does for America.

The Hershey's company is one of the oldest chocolate producers in the USA, and one of American icons thanks to its widely recognizable products, such as Hershey Bars and tear drop shaped chocolate pralines—Hershey Kisses.

Moreover, the Herhey's company is also behind the other very popular chocolate tidbits such as Reese's, and Almond Joy, among others. Being so popular, Herhey's sweets sell in every American grocery store, but Hershey's Times Square location makes it exceptional by itself, plus its interior design and high score in "retailtainment" special features. No wonder this specific place is called the flag (or concept) store of The Greatest American Chocolate Company.

It is one of the most prominent spots on Times Square, riveting the attention of passers-by with its giant 60-foot-wide and 215-foot-tall façade (16 floors), featuring 4,000 chasing lights, 56 neon letters, 30 programmable lights, 14 front-lit signs, four steam machines and other embellishing yet functional props—making it colorful and dazzling.

So, it would be very hard to overlook Herhey's gigantic sweets gift basket at the front, filled with the company's brand products, especially its iconic Herhey's Bar occupying the most honorable central position of this display of honor. Furthermore, this signage technology can also make you an instant Personality of the Day (at least for a few minutes) displaying your name or special message on their exclusive scrolling marquee sign.

The store itself under the colossal, brightly lit display, seems to be surprisingly small, yet it still has enough room for the Original Automatic and Gravitational Chocolate Machine to make the customized mix of candies in a silver bucket of your very own giant Hershey's Kisses.

Immediately, after you enter the place, you are "sweetly" welcomed with a hot chocolate smell. Under the silver, huge candy swirling, there are piles of everything "Herhey's"—from sweets to souvenirs, including unique New York gifts, clothing and toys. The prices are a little higher than in an average grocery store, but Hershey's Time Square is in no way an average store (and it is in Manhattan, anyway). It is the ultimate experience in sweetness at the sweetest place on earth.

If you eat only small portions of sweets or you are on a diet (by all means I do not suspect that you are too thrifty) small Herhey's samples are free. But even for no-carb diet fans, this one-of-a-kind interactive chocolate experience is, simply, priceless.

M&M's World New York

1600 Broadway (at 48th Street)
www.mmsworld.com
🚇Subway directions:
49th Street (N, Q, R)
50th Street (A,C, E, 1, 2)

They talk, they joke, they flirt, they appear on billboards and perform in commercials, so it's quite obvious they have their own store. And taking into account their worldwide popularity, the store couldn't just open anywhere else than in one of the most prestigious addresses in the city and the most crowded tourists destination—Times Square.

It occupies a four-story space at the corner of Broadway, marked with the one of the most visible, colorful and illuminated display in the vicinity, which is a never-ending show with animated M&Ms. Children of all ages (including adults) gawk at the big screen for quite a while.

Inside, there is a real kingdom of the worldwide recognized M&M dragées with hard sugary colorful covers, chocolate filling and, most of all, with a "spirit," which is reinforced by everything M&M, starting with candies in all possible container—tins, jars, mugs, boxes and, unexpectedly, in a gigantic pen, a backpack, a clock, a shoe, fire engine and even in a pillow. But wait! That's not all—there are stuffed animals, you guessed it, filled with M&Ms.

Everywhere in the store, there are vending machines with loose M&M candies and multiple posts to customize M&M orders, from a photo with M&M motif frame to a special box of M&M dragées And, of course, there are candy bars, too. In the wide four-story space, there is enough room for several LED screens continuously presenting M&M related stories and commercials. However, what ultimately matters is a toothsome, chocolaty M&M dragée melting in your mouth. Bon appétit!

Anthropologie

50 Rockefeller Plaza/Rockefeller Center (between 50th and 51st Streets)
www.anthropologie.com
🚇Subway directions:
47th Street-50th Street/Rockefeller Center (B, D, F, M)
5th Avenue-53rd Street (E, M)
49th Street (N, Q, R)

A retail store with its own art gallery? Why not? Especially, if it is situated in Rockefeller Center, one of the most famous city's art and architectural landmarks. The store that proves that is Anthropolgie.

It is one of the three outlets (at least at the time of this writing) of this chain in Manhattan, which offers a rich selection of garment, beauty accessories, and very wide range of home-décor products.

The store in this specific location looks like an antique flea market and an art gallery, showing mostly "cultural anthropology" or "ecology" inspired works under the same roof. The two-floor space comprises eclectic furniture and fixtures, a complete Occitan village-style kitchen, a hunter's living room with the open fireplace with papier-mâché hunting trophies over it, a gigantic "frame" made of books at the entrance, etc.

The artsy and outlandish atmosphere is even more intensified by chipped-paint wooden display tables, cracked ceramics, wrought-iron, blown-glass items and hand-painted oddments placed all around.

Anthropologie, as its name indicates, deals also with anthro-pological themes mixing goods and styles from all over the world—from French rustic to Bali exotic. So, if you want to experience a kind of adventure (or rather "retailventure")—half an hour of shopping in this store is to some degree a quick trip around the world.

Lego Store Rockefeller Center

620 5th Avenue (at 50th Street, Rockefeller Center)
www.stores.lego.com
🚊Subway directions:
47th-50th Streets-Rockefeller Center (B, D, F, M)

There are Lego stores everywhere in the world, but only one has the Big Apple, the Empire State Building, the Statue of Liberty and even the colossal statue of Atlas (lifting the globe)— on the permanent exhibition. All of them represent most recognized New York's landmarks, including the last one which is the visual symbol of the Rockefeller Center itself; and, as you've guessed, they are constructed of Lego blocks, of course.

The store, located in this prestigious area, occupies two floors throughout the corner building with wide glass displays facing towards Rockefeller Plaza with the world-famous golden stature of Mercury and an ice-skating rink in the winter or a café in summer. So it's hard to miss it anyway.

Undoubtedly, it's worth visiting despite being extremely crowded all day long.

There are all kinds of Lego bricks available here, including both the latest designs and classical sets for all those waxing nostalgic souls, or those who like time-proven objects above all else. This Lego emporium offers also blocks packed by the pound, which you can pick from big containers formed into large colorful "legowalls" inside, not without reason called the "Pick-a-Brick Wall" and rare and unique blocks to complete missing parts of old Lego sets or replace damaged ones. Let's not miss the "master builder bar."

This specific Lego store offers even more than bricks, sets and usual Lego stuff. You can buy here educational tools—games, DVDs, and models to enhance creativity, imagination and technical skills as well.

And, because Lego bricks are so easy to assemble and popular through all generations, the store is also a great source of unique gifts in do-it-yourself style, regardless of your age and sense of creativity. Thanks to the simple idea of Lego version of the city's famous landmarks, everybody can take a favorite NYC monument with him or her (such a set fits in even the smallest suitcase) and keep it forever.

NBC Experience Store

30 Rockefeller Plaza (at 49th Street between 5th and 6th Avenues, Rockefeller Center)
www.nbcuniversalstore.com
🚇Subway directions:
47th-50th Streets-Rockefeller Center (B, D, F, M)
49th Street (N, Q, R)
5th Avenue-53rd Street (E, M)

Maybe this is due to the history that started in Rockefeller Center RCA headquarters, or their today's broadcasting studios nearby. Maybe this channel is just more New York than the other ones. Maybe the shows they produce are the most popular among the worldwide audience, or maybe just people like Matt Lauer most than the rest of respectful and likeable TV personalities.

For whatever reason, the fact is that only this one of the public TV channels has its own store in the Midtown Manhattan, often called the Peacock Network (owing to NBC's logo).

Since it is a TV-channel store, large TV screens are placed everywhere in the spacious two-story establishment, conveniently divided into sections connected to all NBC shows: *Friends, Seinfeld, ER, The Office*, and popular children series—*Looney Tunes, Jetsons and Flinstones, Bugs Bunny, Pink Panther*, and *Star Trek* which has its own theme corner shaped like a "real" space station.

Every show are represented by dozens of theme souvenirs and

gadgets. The most recognizable characters and motives are displayed on the screens all around the place so tah you can feel you are in the middle of a busy showroom or TV studio.

So maybe the stuffed Looney Tunes characters are a little bit overpriced (but this is Manhattan), nevertheless, a photo with Matt Lauer (unfortunately, of cardboard, but who will really notice that) can easily compensate all those inconveniences.

Nintendo World

10 Rockefeller Plaza (48th Street between 5th and 6th Avenues, Rockefeller Center)
www.nintendoworldstore.com
🚇Subway directions:
47th-50th Streets-Rockefeller Center (B, D, F, M)

If the most important feature of an "interesting" store is a "shopping experience," then Nintendo World is among the best ones.

This two-story glass cube, fronting on Rockefeller Center Plaza, is packed with all kinds and generations of video game devices, and, of course, the newest, but also classical games to play on the spot, which creates a one-of-a-kind retailtainment heaven.

Apart from shopping attractions, Nintendo World offers a lot of fun for fun's sake: graffiti-style interior design based on the brand popular themes, large LCD screens, rows of gaming machines almost everywhere, hundreds of accessories, garments, and gadgets.

To make more fun, Super Mario and Pikachu welcoming guests at the entrance, the Pokemon world with tons of stuffed creatures representing the "breed," collectable trade cards, the Wii Wonderland upstairs, and even a small museum with all the characters ever created by Nintendo, from Abra to Zelda. And they sell N.Y. Super Mario key chains, too.

McKenzie-Childs

20 W 57th Street (between 5th Avenue and 6th Avenue)
www.mckenzie-childs.com
🚇Subway directions:
57th Street (F)
5th Avenue-59th Street (N, Q, R)

Seeing a chessboard and chess players, you probably think of a game of chess whereas New Yorkers immediately think of McKenzie-Childs store.

They are accustomed to the black and white façade of a townhouse in downtown New York whose all details, including awnings over windows, are designed with a motif of a chessboard—the peculiar trademark of the originators and owners of this place, ceramic artists, Victoria and Richard McKenzie-Childs. They founded it as an art gallery and showroom to present flatware, hand-made tiles, furniture, fabrics, and various artistic knick-knacks. And, although some time ago, somebody else became the owner, it still is in part a store, in part a peculiar art gallery.

In fact, all the building makes the exhibition space and its décor is entirely a work of the artistic couple: from floor tiles, decorations on the walls and ceilings to all the furniture and every, even smallest, detail. The majority of these objects are decorated with the trademark of chessboard, thus everybody can immediately recognize their origin from the studio of McKenzie-Childs.

Frankly, visiting this special place incites, mainly, associations (or even an illusion) of being on "the other side of the mirror"—everything here is seemingly casual like in an ordinary Manhattan brownstone townhouse but at the same time—like in a fairy tale, unreal, even crazy and ludicrous. For instance, ceramic checker-patterned moose's head with gold-plated antlers hung over the fireplace just by a clock framed (you've guessed it) in black and white.

If you visit this Wonderland, you would be amazed like Alice once was, and you will see a world in checkered patterns, and be entranced by this magical place. To better remember this wonderful time, you can buy whatever you like, of course, the moose's head, too.

The Shops at Columbus Circle/Time Warner Center

10 Columbus Circle (at 59th Street between Central Park West and Broadway, Theater District)
www.theshopsatcolumbuscircle.com
🚇Subway directions:
59th Street-Columbus Circle (1,2,A, B, C, D)
57th Street-7th Avenue (N, Q, R)
66th Street-Lincoln Center (1, 2)

The Shops at Columbus Circle, one of the latest city's landmarks, occupy the most prestigious part of its almost 3,000.000-square-foot space, which hosts roughly 40 stores. And all of them seem to be selected because of their visual attraction.

From Armani and Art of Shaving to Williams Sonoma, all the boutiques are not only renowned brands, but also they are arranged as pieces of interior art themselves. In order to keep with the unusual artsy atmosphere of this iconic, contemporary architecture, the display space is constructed from glass and marble, and completed with museum-quality pieces of art by Botero and Indiana among the others.

On the main floor, Williams-Sonoma reigns supreme with upscale kitchen utensils, cookware, tableware, cookbooks, home décor, etc.

The store offers all kitchen necessities from basics to the rare and refined utensils, only the best chefs know what they are for, and they share their knowledge with the store's customers; that's why, WS offers cooking (or rather cuisine) classes on a regular basis, along with all kinds of cookbooks as well.

Martha Stewart lovers' heaven occupies two-story space full of kitchen everything and all this everything of the highest quality is beautifully displayed and packed in artsy and stylized rustic wooden furniture.

Upstairs, there is a small but impressive showroom filled with home furniture arranged as a real home setting, giving plenty of interior-design ideas to carry into effect almost immediately because most of the items on display can be bought.

The basement hosts the largest supermarket in Manhattan—Whole Foods, on its almost 60,000 square feet not only selling every kind of gourmet food imaginable but also offering numerous specialties, unique in the entire city.

Here you can come across a sushi bar with organic seaweed, the enormous coffee aisle with an incredible selection of products along with a 300-seat café, and chocolate enrobing station covering with chocolate everything you want (well, almost everything).

Besides, in that area, there is a flower shop with the walk-in greenhouse full of exotic, rare flowers, and a cosmetics department offering makeover services on the spot, along with free samples of body and beauty products, and even hand-made soap bars. For gourmands and gourmets, there are upscale restaurants, bars, a bakery, and a chocolatier. The latest attraction is C. Wonder's second Manhattan store which is like the original SoHo unit (also in this guide) but this time "on steroids." It has more color and more props, including life-size multicolored striped zebras, dotted horses and six-foot teddy bears. There is also an illuminated gateway at the entrance with LED lights.

The Shops on Columbus Circle host various fashion and cultural events.

So, if somebody is looking for a New York style shopping experience, there is no better destination in the entire city than this previous Time Warner Building location.

And the view form here over Central Park and the Columbus Monument is an additional, unforgettable and one-of-a-kind attraction.

All she is missing is a big shopping bag...in The Shops at Columbus Circle

MIDTOWN EAST

Fifth Avenue from 34th Street up is...the Fifth Avenue because this name stands for a symbol of upscale haute couture by itself—only this time, enriched by flagships of more popular international brands: H&M, Gap, Guess, JCP, Diesel, Dsquared or Juicy Couture, to name just a few. Near 57th Street, there are Henri Bendel, Versace, Chanel, Dior, Vuitton, Armani, Prada, Cartier, Burberry and Tiffany & Co. signature stores, all of them within a one-mile radius. Undoubtedly, when it comes to shopping, Midtown East is the most popular destination while in the New York.

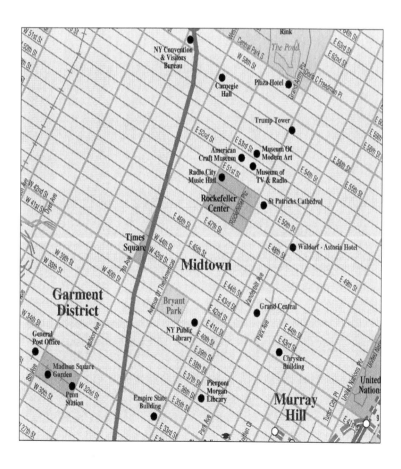

Pleasingly dizzying stairs in Armani's store at Fifth Avenue

Dover Street Market

160 Lexington Avenue (between 30th and 31st Streets)
www.newyork.doverstreetmarket.com
🚃Subway directions:
33rd Street (4, 6)

You cannot find Dover Street anywhere in New York City. However, a market with this name opened on Lexington Avenue a few years ago, in the former building of a design school. It looks like everything you can imagine except one— a high fashion store. For instance, you can't do window shopping here as there are no windows in grey limestone walls. What's more, the store has no permanent interior décor, either. Of course, you can spot here and there an unchanging element of the store's architecture, including Niki de St. Phalle-style staircase and a chimney-like glass elevator shaft leading from the first floor up to the very ceiling.

All the other space arrangements are really ephemeral, remodeled at least twice a year.

That's why, DSM, unlike most other retail outlets in the city, closes for renovation for a couple of weeks before every winter and summer season.

So, it's like visiting a quite a new store twice a year at the same location. And, of course the collections are also thoroughly changed. The renovation breaks bring significant losses to the business, but who cares, when fashion is considered as art here.

The founder and owner of this unusual place Rei Kawakubo and famous designer and long-standing art director of Commes des Garçons, takes care of almost every detail in the store and creates the best possible setting for her unique sculpture-like clothes. Of course, the place hosts also other vanguard fashion designers, such as Alexander Wang, Raf Simons, Junya Watanabe, and Rick Owens, to name a few.

The prices here for upmarket clothes and accessories are obviously high, but the store is worth visiting not only for the joy of shopping but also for a simple pleasure of being in the place that is a piece of art itself.

It represents one of the best examples of „impossible architecture" ever built. Each of its seven floors is like a page of the never-written second part of Alice in Wonderland, only instead of Alice, this time it's all about Rei, the designer. And every fashionista knows that the entrance to the Enchanted World is not somewhere in the Rabbit Hole, but just around the corner of 160 Lexington Avenue and 30th Street in Manhattan.

Reebok CrossFit 5th Avenue

420 5th Avenue (between 38th and 37th Streets)
www.reebokcrossfit5thave.com
🚇Subway directions:
5th Avenue (7)
34th Street-Herald Square (B, D, F, M, N, Q, R)

Many stores in New York try to offer not only a wide selection of good-quality merchandise at a decent price, but also" a good shopping experience; nevertheless only a few succeed, among them—Reebok Crossfit 5th Avenue, a Fit Hub Concept store. It is the first, and so far the largest store of this kind in the USA, which, according to its CEO, "is not exactly a gym, and isn't exactly a store since it's actually an experience."

This is the place where you can go shopping for sport gear and accessories, or you can have a workout in the CrossFit Box gym in the basement, filled with all kinds of equipment—both very basic and highly advanced, so you can choose the most appropriate for you.

As the CrossFit esthetics is, by definition, "functional but raw and natural," so is the entire store, with exposed beams and ceilings, recycled rubber flooring, plywood boxes and tires throughout the place. The staff are not only experts in the merchandise offered here, but they are also fitness consultants.

So every item bought in the store could be easily tested on the spot, in one of the colorful CrossFit boxes downstairs.

Brooks Brothers

346 Madison Avenue (between 44th and 45th Streets)
www.brooksbrothers.com
🚇Subway directions:
Grand Central-42nd Street (2, 5, 6)
5th Avenue (7)

This two-century store on Madison Avenue has been the oldest men's garment establishment in America since 1818. When it was founded by Henry Sand Brooks, followed by his five sons, the Brooks Brothers, and it is was the first store in America to introduce Oxford button-downs (in, ready-made suits, and, a hundred years later, legendary "non-iron" shirts (still in stock, by the way). From its beginnings in downtown Manhattan, the brand bet on the "classics that never go out of style," choosing up-to-date, but never extravagant novelties.

Brooks Brothers' famous clientele list includes tycoon J.P. Morgan, aviation pioneer Charles Lindberg, novelist Scott Fitzgerald, and actor Clark Gable. Furthermore, the store was a preferred garment supplier of Abraham Lincoln (as well as other US presidents), and when he was shot, even then, he was wearing a Brooks Brothers suit.

Two centuries later this giant flagship store, furnished with dark-wood furniture and panels, with stylish chandeliers, still offers Shetland sweaters, good-quality, classically cut suits, Harris tweeds, madras, polo and golf supplies "to die for," memorabilia as well as women's and kid's collections.

After entering the store you feel like being in a British gentlemen club because of its atmosphere and interior design. The place is filled with the highest quality clothes and accessories, and it remains faithful to the principles of its founders, not only paying tribute to the noble past and classic elegance, but keeping up with the present. So gentlemen can visit a bedroom and a studio, furnished and designed in sophisticated elegant Upper-West-Side style, and ardent golfers can have fun with indoor PGA simulator and play virtual golf (almost like in a real tournament), which is probably the only device of this kind in a retail store worldwide.

The Art of Shaving

373 Madison Avenue (between 45th and 46th Streets)
www.theartofshaving.com
🚇Subway directions:
Grand Central -42nd Street (4, 5, 6,)
5th Avenue (7)

Since everything in New York can be an art—why not the art of experiencing something, say, shaving? And, here it is, at Madison Avenue, exactly The Art of Shaving, offering both shaving stuff and experience (the extreme one, almost). Just image a scene like the one in the movie *Le Chien Andalou*: a crazy barber armed with a cut-throat razor approaches you...and it's really happening in AS all the time (without the cutting, of course) where, at the back of the store, stylized as an early 19th-century barber parlor, there is a real barber spot with an antique barber chair covered with brown quilted leather.

So, before buying some shaving cosmetics and accessories at the front of the store, everybody can test the stuff taking part or just watching the elaborated, old-fashioned art of shaving.

And, after that, you he can soothe his nerves in a small but elegant men's spa, the only really modern part of this old time-masculine-looking place, with walls covered with dark wood, dark quilted leather club sofas and chairs, traditional barber utensils displayed on dark wood drawer chests, framed old photographs, and antique razors in glass cases hanging all over the walls.

Entering the interior, saturated with genuine cologne scent, is just like traveling through time, coming back to those years before Bics and electric razors were invented.

The store inventory, among other things, consists of authentic badger brushes, wet-shaving razors, old-style shaving soaps (coming in tubes) and fine colognes, as well as up-to-date moisturizers, lotions, face masks and other high-quality men's cosmetics.

The same assortment is offered by the other Art of Shaving chain outlets in different New York locations; however, exclusively this one serves also as an old-time barber parlor.

This is the only place in the city to convince all Gillette users that shaving is also an art.

Build-a-Bear Workshop

565 Fifth Avenue (at 46th Street)
www.buildabear.com
🚇Subway directions:
47th-50th Streets/Rockefeller Center (B, D, F, M)
5th Avenue (7)
Grand Central -42nd Street (S)

The first Build-A-Bear Workshop opened in Saint Louis in 1997, and since then it has been mushrooming throughout the world, numbering now more than 400 stores, which have already sold more than 70 million teddy bears. The New York branch of the chain is the largest, and that's why, it has earned the status of the flagship. The other reason is that president Theodore Roosevelt, who was born in New York, is the "godfather" of all teddy bears ever stuffed. In fact, the bear was named after him in the early years of the 20th century, instantly becoming an iconic toy.

Only in this store, you can buy NYPD Teddy, NY Fire Teddy, and Yankee Monkey, or Liberty Bear, among others.

A part of the store's name is "workshop" because it not only sells different kinds of stuffed animals but also "brings them to life". Some of stuffed bears and other creatures "are born" on the spot according to customers' designs; you or your kid choose—say—pelage, ears, eyes (options are innumerable), and then the newborn bear is being assembled and stuffed, sorry, is born. Eventually, after adding the finishing touches, the bear receives the "heart" during a so-called "heart ceremony." All those furry creatures, including rather smooth Hello Kitties, are given their names and unique birth certificates.

Usually no bear is bare (no pun intended) here; they are dressed up in colorful costumes, cute booties and fancy accessories.

Actually, the outfits give them an appearance you may look for, as for instance Harley-Davidson Bear, Cinderella Bear, Cowboy Bear, Hawaiian Bear, and naturally, Mickey Mouse Bear.

Besides all the fun to design a unique toy and hours of choosing clothes and accessories for it, the Build-a-Bear Workshop is the only store in New York to buy something with the heart. Besides an "I love New York" T-shirt or mug, of course.

American Girl Place
609 5th Avenue (between 48th and 49th Streets)
www.americangirlplace.com
🚇Subway directions:
5th Avenue-53rd Street (E, M)
47th-50th Streets/Rockefeller Center (B, D, F, M)
51st Street (4, 6)

Since in New York there is a shop for everybody, there must be the one for doll lovers, too. In fact, AGP pretends to be mostly for the dolls themselves; however, as long as they don't use Visa Platinum credit cards the store is for girls—of any age and not only American, of course.

The midtown doll emporium under the rose sunshades looks like a gigantic playhouse and includes a spa with a hair stylist salon, a studio of photography, a theater, a restaurant serving lunches, tea and dinners, and—just in the end of all these facilities— the store itself selling dolls and accessories for them.

So, since the place is mostly about playing and buying girls' favorite toys, everything here invites everybody to have fun, from the hair salon offering novelties in dolls coiffures to the restaurant with special chairs and tableware for these unusual but welcomed guests. Even the photo studio is well prepared for the girls and their dolls who can have "family" pictures here. This way of shopping and looking for new " friends" and their accessories is also a good occasion to socialize, to participate in a music show, to have lunch or dinner.

This store is not only for girls and dolls. It's also for boys, mostly grown-up, who love their girls and dolls enough to pay a significant price for that one-of-a-kind shopping experience.

Ted Baker Grand House

595 5th Avenue (at 48th Street)
www.tedbaker.com
🚇Subway directions:
5th Avenue-59th Street (R, Q)

What kind of store could be hidden behind a window display, almost completely filled with a gigantic grandpa's clock with all these cogged-wheels, scales, chains and gears in motion? A garment store, of course. If only it represents everything London as does Ted Baker Grand House. It seems to be obvious then that the interior doesn't look like a store, well, a typical store; it rather looks as if it were a stylish London townhouse jointly owned by Sherlock Holmes and Alice from Wonderland.

The art-deco staircase, red-brick walls, dark wood paneling, velvet curtains and club furniture are very "Sherlockesque," but the dining table setting along the register counter, tea pots and cups, ceiling lamps and jello lighting, and, of course, chessboard tiling along the walls and oval mirrors framed with dark wood can come from no one else's place than that one of Alice's.

In such an establishment, wellies and umbrellas must be the most important accessories, nevertheless, Ted Baker offers the full inventory of "luxury designed goods at affordable prices," including everything from elegant women's dresses to whimsical men's ties. This is then one of the best places to play Alice shopping in Wonderland named New York.

Saks Fifth Avenue

611 5th Avenue (between 51st and 52nd Streets)
www.saksfifthavenue.com
🚇Subway directions:
5th Avenue/53rd Street (E, M)
47th-50th Streets/Rockefeller Center (B, D, F, M)
51st Street (4, 6)

Where to go if somebody needs wardrobe or wedding consulting, messenger service, package delivery or restaurant and theatre reservation, not to mention an afternoon tea and spa, all at once? In Manhattan, there is no other answer than Saks Fifth Avenue.

Furthermore, the store offers 10 floors of designer merchandise, including the second (after Macy's) largest shoe department in the entire city, which is probably the only retail outlet in the world that has its own postal zip code 10022-SHOE.

The lower floors of this upscale, luxury emporium hosts 23 of the most prestigious fashion designers in the boutiques—from "A" as in Armani to "V" as in Louis Vuitton. If you plan to buy something here, don't forget to take a big wad of money or a platinum credit card with you because the prices here are usually four-digit a piece; for example, a ritzy Italian Kiton suit costs some 7,000 dollars.

Fortunately, on the highest carpeted marble floors, you can find something less pricey, but still coming from renown brands, including Juicy Couture and Marc Jacobs, among others.

Saks Fifth Avenue offers a huge selection of products: classy lingerie, jewelry, handbags, cosmetics, swanky furs, even exquisite home furnishing—you name it, you've got it.

The store opened in 1924, which makes it one of the oldest

upscale retail landmarks in New York. After the last renovation, its interior looks amazing—filled with white Carrera marble, grey wood, crystal chandeliers, antique mirrors, and vintage furniture—all that in wide open spaces in warm, light tones, highlighted by metallic upholstery, custom-made modern tables and chairs, futuristic lighting, a hand-blown Murano glass, and artsy wall centerpiece on the eighth floor, not to mention state-of-the-art computer terminals throughout the entire store, and a one-of-a-kind chocolate fountain and a gorgeous chandelier above a curved counter in the Charbonnel et Walker Chocolate Café on the same floor (serving its famous Sticky Toffee Chocolate Pudding and Apple Crumble). The store's famous Christmas windows and façade luminous snowflake decorations are just a cherry on the top.

Zara

666 5ᵗʰ Avenue (between 52nd and 53rd Streets)
www.zara.com
🚇Subway directions:
5th Avenue-53rd Street (E, M)
57th Street (F)
5th Avenue-59th Street (N, Q, R)

Zara, the well-established Spanish-origin world retailer, famous for its "fast-fashion" affordable clothing, holds currently eight outlets in New York. The largest of them (also the largest in the US) is located on Manhattan's famed Fifth Ave. It is a so-called "new-concept global store", being not a replica of typical Zara shops, but a store with a new interior design, representing a new philosophy of retailing. According to the company, the store's décor is based on four principles: beauty, clarity, functionality and sustainability, while the brand philosophy is affordable luxury.

The 32,000-square-foot space on three floors in the historic Tishman Building is arranged in a very well-thought-out manner.

In the central part of the store, there is gigantic Cannes-style staircase with mannequins as if on catwalks presenting the latest fashion trends (the store refreshes their merchandise twice a week). The corridors flanking the staircase lead shoppers to alcove-like boutiques on either side, each with different fashion collection.

To make the navigation easier, the store employs the system of black lines on white floors and ceiling lighting "following" the customers. The store's interior holds mostly glass, resin and stripped aluminum finish (usually black and white), and wooden furniture as well as brownish steel rack—making the place simple, clear, but first of all, functional and beautiful at the same time.

In many respects, it looks like a more spacious version of Calvin Klein's (CK) flagship store on Madison Ave.

The biggest difference between those two outlets is that Zara offers luxury which is supposed to be affordable even far from Fifth Avenue.

Hollister

668 5th Avenue (between 52nd and 53rd Streets) and
600 Broadway (between Prince and Houston Streets)
www.hollister.com
🚇Subway directions:
5th Avenue (7)
Bryant Park-42nd Street (B, D, F, M)

When in the middle of a cold and wet dusk in midtown Manhattan, suddenly there appears something as incredible as a hot and sunny California beach (Huntington Beach, to be precise), it does not necessarily mean a mirage, triggered by overwhelming, all-pervasive and monotonous structures of granite and glass skyscrapers.

It's just Hollister—a Californian all-year-round summer enclave under the leaden Manhattan winter sky. The Beach is, indeed, virtual, and you can enjoy it only through a live video transmission shown on 180-inch flat panels mounted on this

Manhattan flagship store's façade. Moreover, the infinity edge pools of running water in front of the enormous screen look surprisingly real.

The experience of Californian beaches is even more complete in the first of New York Hollister flagship stores in SoHo, offering casual clothes and preserving its "surfing theme park" identity not only because of the interior architecture but also because of hiding everything deeply in the dark, which makes it probably the dimmest retail space in the city. The four-story boardwalk inside, surrounded by multiple "fishing cabins," and the central wood and iron footbridge-style staircase seem to be almost real, all the more so that TV panels all around imitate windows with a view over the sea.

Loud music, gigantic plants, an intensive cologne scent and plenty of young and comely staff in shorts and bikinis make this flabbergasting experience more authentic. Actually, even if most of the jeans, shorts, T-shirts and flip-flop are hardly visible; any question to the sales assistants rather won't be heard (although they are all very well-mannered), and the fitting rooms are plunged into darkness, those "obstacles" seem to be worth the final effect—a unique shopping experience— which is hard to forget for many reasons, including darkness and noise. And anything else is easy to order online.

Uniqlo

666 5th Avenue (at 53rd Street)
www.uniqlo.com
🚇Subway directions:
5th Avenue-53rd Street (E, M)
57th Street (F)
47th-50th Street/Rockefeller Center (B, D, F, M)

Numbers don't lie— there are almost 90,000 square feet of retail space here, which is a record-breaking size for this chain throughout the world, and makes this place, at least for a while, the largest store on the entire Fifth Avenue. It has that all: 100 fitting rooms, 50 cash registers, 350 dummies, more than 400 LED displays and video columns, glass elevators with a view over the street, gigantic three-story high escalator, futuristic glass tunnel, glass "bridge," two staircases with rainbow panels and even "magic mirrors" changing the garment color with a touch on the screen. It seems to be enough to create an impressive "window to the world" for the popular Japanese brand—Uniqlo, even in such a competitive location as Fifth Avenue in Midtown, Manhattan. No to mention, this specific "window' attracts passers-by with its three-story glass and LED façade.

In this case bigger does mean better—not only in store design, which makes a significant difference in " retailtainment" quality, but also in the merchandise selection. This outlet offers everything—from the classic lines to the brand newest collections, and, by the way, that Fifth Avenue flagship store is the only place in the city where you can buy signature T-shirts from Uniqlo designers.

No wonder the store attracts not only fans of this original Japanese brand since the place offers Unique Clothes and a unique shopping show as well.

Tommy Hilfiger

681 Fifth Avenue (between 53rd and 54th Street)
www.tommy.com
🚇Subway directions:
5th Avenue-53rd Street (E, M)
5th Avenue-59th Street (N, R, Q)

The shortest definition of Tommy Hilfiger's style came from the designer himself during his interview with VMSD—"A fun take on Americana, classic yet sophisticated." And this so-called "global flagship" is the clear evidence of his words. This is the place where modern architecture meets traditional one. In this case "modern" means the spectacular, spiral white ribbon, Guggenheim-Museum-like staircase, which faces towards Fifth Avenue from the side of the original, all-glass and limestone façade of the former Fortunoff building (very thoroughly restored). Whereas "traditional" stands for an unusual interior design compiled from the "Americanas": pieces of furniture, gadgets, lamps and popular products referring to, or just representing so-called "American icons."

So, besides the classy bronze fixtures, walnut paneling and Venini chandeliers, the entire store is filled with taxidermy squirrels and stags, preserved butterflies, vintage leather suitcases, an antique motorbike, archaic "Vogue" magazines, hand-painted saucers, old car license plates, vinyl records, handmade quilts and other stuff representing an extensive collection of '80s American kitsch. However, the most important element of the "traditional" part of the store décor is the 50-foot art wall featuring the Tommy Hilfiger red and white flag logo.

All the above-mentioned objects define the spirit of Hilfiger's brand and collections. Saying "collections," I mean every imaginable bit of Tommy: clothing, footwear, and recently, swanky eveningwear—for all age groups and genders. You can be sure that shopping in the Tommy Hilfiger flagship will be nearly as enjoyable as visiting the Folk Art Museum nearby.

Polo Ralph Lauren
711 5th Avenue (at 55th Street)
🚇Subway directions:
5th Avenue-53rd Street (E, M)

It's hard to believe that one of the most easily recognizable fashion brands throughout the world, existing for more than half a century, did not have its flagship store on Fifth Avenue for five decades. Fortunately, it's no longer the case, at least since 2014 when the first ever Ralph Lauren Polo store opened in Midtown, Manhattan, in the historic building, erected at the corner of Fifth Avenue and 55th Street in 1927.

The three-story interior, covered in oak and stone, is a good mark of everything that according to Ralph Lauren, the

designer and founder of the company, makes his Polo style—
"timeless elements of classic elegance ... and an aspirational
lifestyle that has come to define the essence of the company."

On the flagship's 38,000-squre-foot area, there are the
trendiest Polo collections, of clothing and accessories for all
gender and age groups, and, for the first time in the company's
history, tea and coffee. Just only in this store of the chain is
Ralph's Coffee bar serving its own brand coffee in white cups
with the green PRL logo. Its interior décor matches the
architecture of the whole: traditional wooden chairs are placed
around an oval cream-colored sofa and small round tables.

The retail space of PRL seems to be a blend of the rustic style
of the American Interior and the austere New York brick-and-
mortar design. Next to white simple display cases and very
sleek modern lighting, there are four fire places covered with
river stones and many and many elements of the décor belong
to American material culture of the early 20th century, such as
black and white photographs of Manhattan, collections of
classical guitars, vintage motorbikes, bicycles, and clocks, and
even kayaks (one of them, colored in indigo, is hanging bottom-
up from the ceiling).

All this creates a welcoming ambience, but if you feel a little
tired after a shopping marathon through all three floors, you
can stop by the Polo Bar & Restaurant, which is located right
next to the store. Here you can take a breather, browse your
receipts, and just relax while sitting on a leather sofa and
relishing the taste of Ralph's Coffee Ice Cream.

Armani Fifth Avenue
715 5th Avenue (between 55th and 56th Streets)
www.armani5thavenue.com
🚆Subway directions:
5th Avenue and 53rd Street (E, M)
57th Street (F)
5th Avenue-59th Street (N, Q, R)

Even not being a New York fashionista, everybody knows what the brand Armani stands for. Suffice to say Armani/5th Avenue store offers just Armani-everything. Four floors of two Midtown buildings, transformed into the flagship Armani's store by the Massimilliano and Doriana Fukas in 2007-2009, sells all the designer's lines and collections.

The store does not contain only fashion commodities but also a gourmet restaurant and café (Armani Dolce) serving mouthwatering desserts that deliciously complete this unique shopping experience. AFA has outstanding architecture, being paved with dark marble and covered with black false ceilings, and vertical, glass façades with a spectacular view of Midtown Manhattan busy street life through the translucent walls.

However, the most remarkable part of the store design seems to be the white, spiral staircase , similar to the most famous of all staircases of that kind, from the Guggenheim Museum. This amazing piece of art occupies the four-story open space of Armani Fifth Avenue interior, just in the middle of the building structure.

Armani is one of the most prestigious names in the fashion world. The spiral staircase is the most prominent feature in his flagship store. So the better way to feel like a Broadway diva is, as you've already guessed it, is just stepping down these stairs (naturally flooded with lights and applause), with an Armani brand signature bag in hand, to the best possible effect.

Dolce & Gabbana

715 5thAvenue (between 55th and 56th Streets)
www.dolcegabbana.com
Subway directions:
5th Avenue/53rd Street (E, M)

The stretch of Fifth Avenue between 60th and 60th streets is regarded as a luxury symbol, which translates into sky-high prices, superior quality and prestige. All this needs an adequate setting, so it's not surprising that the most upmarket stores occupy former local aristocrats' mansions, as for example, Ralph Lauren's fashion houses at Madison Avenue. (in this guide on pages 142 and 143).

If this kind of building is not available, designers go to no end of trouble in order to make luxurious store interiors look like luxurious mansions, once belonging to the Rockefellers or Vanderbilts.

Entering such establishments, you immediately notice marble floors, marble wall ornaments, and—spectacular marble staircases, which are the hallmark of Manhattan upscale stores.

Their interiors are distinguished by large uncluttered spaces, a spectacular staircase and minimalist elegant décor. And such is the new flagship of Dolce & Cabana.

However, there is smoothing that distinguishes its interior— it's a huge chandelier, made in Italian Baroque style, whose entire structure is black with crystal-like glass beads forming garlands and pendants. It's the most distinctive décor item in this place, hanging right over the floor in the center of the store (no pun intended).

Such items as the chandelier are in contradiction with New York minimalism in décor, but perfectly complete it.

By the same token, it would be hard to miss large crystal mirrors in intricately carved gold-plated frames and balustrade. The very staircase triggers associations with opera because of the way of displaying the latest D&G's collections, that is, in open cases on the intermediate floors (mezzanines). Also, velvet sofas, glossy brown wooden cabinets and display tables on the second and third floors furnished in nouveau rich Sicilian style.

This kind of esthetics is rarity in Manhattan, which makes it intriguing, and, to some extent, attractive and tempting like everything that's unusual.

This is the way, the Italian designer duo, as part of cultural diversity, tutor us in Italian fashion and life in the very heart of Manhattan.

Sony Store/Sony Wonder Technology Lab

550 Madison Avenue (at 55th Street)
www.store.sony.com
🚇Subway directions:
5th Avenue-53rd Street (E, M)
5th Avenue- 59th Street (N, Q, R)
59th Street (4, 5, 6)

A s is known, buying a VAIO notebook or a PlayStation online is the most convenient and customer-preferable way to do so.

However, geeks usually want to get their hands on real stuff, which in their case means "touching is believing." The best place to have this sensory experience is Sony Store at Madison Avenue. It is not just another Sony-style place in NYC, but it is more like Sony Island on Manhattan Island with Sony everything: brand-name computers, tablets, TVs, phones, camcorders, and games consoles (in a special Playsation Lounge) as well as Sony Plaza and Sony Wonder Technology Lab—a kind of laboratory and science museum in one, presenting complex technology in simple and fun ways. Here you can talk to a robot (mostly giving him commands and instructions), take pictures of snowflakes, play Muve interactive games, or perform a virtual open-heart surgery.

Fans of visual media or aspiring movie directors can participate in broadcasting and recording experiments and performances. The place also features a small IMAX theater, and a Starbucks café, with comfortable chairs everywhere. All that creates a welcoming atmosphere and a nice meeting spot (naturally, with WiFi).

So, there is a lot of Sony fun here, even if you don't buy a tablet or any other gadget made by that multinational conglomerate corporation. And you, of course, even if you don't like the corporate world at all.

Abercrombie & Fitch

720 5th Avenue (between 56th and 57th Streets)
www.abercrombie.com
🚇Subway directions:
5th Avenue-53rd Street (E, M)
5th Avenue-59th Street (N, Q, R)
57th Street (F)

In New York, there are retail stores easy to mistake with art galleries, theme exhibitions, historic site museums, craft workshops and the like. So it is nothing unusual for the place which is more like a night club than a mere chain retailer. Who, being in the middle of a busy tourist day in Manhattan, wants to melt into the crowd of youngsters and really loud music, can do it easily stopping by the 5th Avenue Abercrombie & Fitch flagship store.

The interior of this youth fashion emporium looks rather like an upscale, two-hundred-year-old library because of its solid dark wood shelves and display tables, bronze fixtures and murals running from the basement to the fourth floor ceiling. However, instead of reading, the young men feature various "states of undress," and rather than studying, they are engaged in activities typical for an Ivy League prep summer camp.

Anyway, this does not bother anybody since the store interior is pretty dark, even on sunny days, so all the elegant, library-like décor is hardly visible, by contrast with the wide LED panels with attractive young models in A&F's newest collections of casual wear for its 18-22-year-old target customers. And since the youngsters need no words to communicate their obvious fashion needs and expectations, there is hardly possible to hear even one's own thoughts here because of the very loud music inside.

It may be a part of a sophisticated method to keep the older generations away from the A&F stores as it has been scientifically proven that only really young persons can easily stand such a noise longer than for half an hour. And they obviously do. The A&F store is the only place miles away from any direction in Manhattan with a long line at the entrance almost all the time. The brand is really famous, especially among tourists, and the A&F became a New York symbol somehow despite its Californian origin.

Maybe, also, young beautiful models in skimpy clothes looking like Greek gods and goddesses, greeting the crowd at the main entrance have something to do with that popularity.

Tiffany & Co

727 5th Avenue (between 56th and 57th Streets)
www.tiffany.com
🚇Subway directions:
5th Avenue-59th Street (N, Q, R)
5th Avenue-53rd Street (E, M)
57th Street (F)

Even though there are countless places serving excellent breakfast in Manhattan, the best of the best still remains the "Breakfast at Tiffany's," anyway.

The store, operating at the current location since 1940, has appeared in the US National Register of Historic Places as one of the more distinctive landmarks, and as such it meets the expectations through its limestone and polished granite Art Deco style façade with a nine-foot tall bronze Atlas shouldering a clock, Alpine marble 124,000-square-foot interior with breathtaking chandeliers, private selling salons with platinum ceilings, and even the Tiffany's Co. Archives.

However, much more impressive are the diamonds, kept in glass and cherry-wood showcases and displayed in all their glory using a unique lighting system. Among them is the most famous and precious, 126-carat Tiffany Diamond exhibited in the mezzanine salon—a museum-like exclusive gallery of company's most spectacular jewelry, diamonds, and rare gemstones, which are created to be "the ultimate expression of Tiffany's great traditions and a symbol of nearly 175-year relationship with the city." In the nearby atelier, customers can participate in the one-of-a-kind jewelry creation process, and learn about the history of horology (art of designing and making clocks) at the in-store Patek-Phillipe showcase salon, presenting a permanent collection of unique horological masterpieces (borrowed from the Patek Philippe Museum in Geneva), including the Chronograph and Perpetual Calendar with platinum case and 36 displayed diamonds.

Since the great majority of jewelry sold here may trigger off "sticker shock," the store provides a collection of much less expensive items, such as key chains and money clips.

So everybody can leave this place with a Tiffany signature blue box, introduced in 1837, its first year of operation in Manhattan. Bearing in mind that no breakfast tastes better than Tiffany's Breakfast in New York.

Niketown

6 E 57th Street (between 5th and Madison Avenues)
www.nike.com
🚊Subway directions:
5th Avenue-59th Street (N, Q, R)
5th Avenue-53rd Street (E, M)
57th Street (F)

If an activewear lovers' and sport enthusiasts' heaven somewhere exists, it must be Niketown because this Midtown megastore has athlete's everything, from basics to the hardest to find and custom-made sneakers as well.

However, this five-story sportswear emporium offers not only the widest selection of sport items possible to imagine, but also it is worth sightseeing as one of the best examples of creative architecture and interior design applied to a retail outlet in the city.

The building is architecturally very unusual ; It is a hybrid which consists of two different edifices formed like a ship in a bottle: the "bottle" is the exterior structure with the façade, which is stylized as an old, early 20th century New York gymnasium whereas "the ship" is the interior, completely free-standing, ultra-modern concrete building with five floors of Nike everything over the central atrium gallery space.

The almost undecorated interior, made from wood and brick, is filled mostly with shelves and display tables with sneakers and T-shirts arranged in such a way that can be easily mistaken for contemporary art installations. The picture is perfectly completed with gigantic LCD panels.

It is probably the only store in NYC where products are treated like a precious sculptures, as are the Nike sneakers from the newest collection, exhibited at the store entrance on the spotlighted gallery-style white plinths. There is no doubt what kind of "art," is being worshiped here.

This place is, beyond any doubt, the most prominent and trendsetting "body art" gallery in the city.

Bergdorf Goodman

754 5th Avenue (between 57th and 58th Streets)
www.berdorfgoodman.com
🚇Subway directions:
5th Avenue-59th Street (N, Q, R)
57th Street (F)
5th Avenue-53rd Street (E, M)

This hundred-year-old luxury department store became famous not only for being one of the city's antique retail establishments. The glorious past of Vanderbilt mansion with the view of the Plaza Hotel and Central Park from its rooms on the highest floors, upscale restaurant, John Barrett's salon and spa, seems not to matter, as well. And even the elegant store boutiques of such couture stars as Narciso Rodriguez, YSL or Jean Paul Gaultier, to name just a few, are not enough (once it was the fur department that made Bergdorf Goodman famous).

Why? Because the memorable question from the movie "How to Marry a Millionaire," was answered: "the gentlemen you meet at the cold cuts counter may not be that attractive as the one you meet in the mink department in Bergdorf's," and since then, several generations of women worldwide have known where to shop to spot a millionaire, and to marry him, eventually.

Bergdorf Goodman is one of the most luxurious and beautiful retail stores in the city, and yet affordable because of its famous sales and "the best kept New York fashion secret"—the fifth floor, offering the most preferable and relatively less expensive brands, from Marc by Marc Jacobs and Theory to DKNY. This is the BG's little tribute to the company's history. The store was the first outlet that introduced ready-to-wear fashion from Paris famous couturiers to America in 1914.

This store is also a perfect example of favorite American stories about going from rags to riches as one of the store owners, Edwin Goodman, first worked for Herman Bergdorf as an apprentice, but in just two years he became the company's co-owner and, not long afterward, the only owner of Bergdorf Goodman.

Since then the store has been playing a successful role as a model example of upscale New York retailer, not only because of the reasons mentioned above but also wide and diverse assortment of luxury products by the world first-league designers. And, of course, it is still the best place to meet (and maybe marry) a local millionaire.

FAO Schwarz
767 5th Avenue (at 58th Street)
www.faoschwarz.com
🚇Subway directions:
5th Avenue-59th Street (Q, N, R)

FAO Schwarz was founded in 1862 under the name "Toy Bazaar" in Baltimore by German immigrant and his brothers. Eight years later, he opened Schwarz Toy Bazaar in New York. Since then, the store has changed its location and owners many times, and eventually, after moving to its current place in the General Motors Building, behind the Apple Store. it has become a flagship store.

Now, together with Toys "R" Us, Inc. (current owner), it's hard to imagine how much more amazing it is. Although not the largest toy emporium in the world, it's still the most famous place of its kind, predominantly because of its important role in the movie *Big* (T. Hanks starred in it), which popularized it tremendously. However, even without the movie, it justly derives acclaim.

When entering the store, real-life Toy-Soldiers warmly greet you and readily pose (with you, if you want) for a keepsake photo. The store is full of colorful plush stuffed animals, all kinds of less or more animated toys and all imaginable sorts of candy—for those with a sweet tooth.

Here, you can buy the latest electronic toy gadgetry. To safeguard its best traditions, FAO Schwarz sells also "classical" teddy bears, wooden blocks and miniature trains. Apart from toys and candy, the store offers many other attractions, including Breakfast with a Toy Soldier at the larger-than-life, really, really Big Piano (as seen in the movie) and even a Store Tour led (yes, you've guessed it!) by an Official FAO Schwarz Toy Soldier, which is suited for children ages three and up and can accommodate groups of 4-30 visitors; so called "personal shoppers" can assist you throughout the tour, upon request. To schedule those services, you can call (212)644-9400 or e-mail partyplanning@fao.com.

Unfortunately, the famous, two-story animated clock is no longer there (but its Face on the elevator still remains at the back of the store).

Other than that, everything in FAO Schwarz creates an unforgettable atmosphere of a fairy tale, or, if you wish, Alice's Wonder(Manhattan)land.

Apple Store

767 5th Avenue (at 59th Street)
www.apple.com/retail/fifthavenue
🚇Subway directions:
5th Avenue-59th Street (N, Q, R)
57th Street (F)
5th Avenue-53rd Street (E, M)

Paris has its glass pyramid in the Louvre courtyard, and New York has its own version of this antique architectural structure, as well. This time it marks the entrance to the sanctuary of what New York is mostly about—the newest technology. And, it is not cone-shaped.

This one is just another cube like the surrounding skyscrapers. In fact, the glass structure with a gigantic silver apple (with a bite taken out of it) figure inside is the only part visible above the sidewalk level at the most famous and crowded Apple store in the city. The rest of it is sunken, like a part of a Manhattan subway system, deep under the ground.

The spiral staircase covered by the glass cube leads down to the large open-space store interior offering "iEverything" (including iPhones®, iPads®, of course).

It's open around the clock so that the most ardent Apple fans could buy their favorite "iSomething" in here conveniently around 2 a.m. Being enormously crowded as the modern architecture masterpiece, the Apple store located in the center of the city, seems to have an additional special mission here. The place is hard to overlook.

So not only ardent Apple fans, can take a small iBite of Big Apple, too.

Argosy Book Store

116 E 59th Street (between Park and Lexington Avenues)
www.argosybooks.com
🚇Subway directions:
59th Street (4, 5, 6)
Lexington Avenue-59th Street (N, R)

Since the word „argosy" means a big cargo ship under the same ownership, this unique store could not be named any better.

The bookstore, one of the rare New York oldtimers, was established in 1925, and it is still operated by the same family. And as the time passed by, this midtown townhouse became a real merchant ship, with its six stories from floors to ceilings filled with antique, rare, printed books, maps and posters, some as old as two hundred years, dated back to the 18th century.

The second meaning of the store name comes from „Argo," a mythological vessel of the Argonauts, trying to find the Golden Fleece, the ancient equivalent for today's Fort Knox treasury content.

And Argosy has its own treasure too, as the well kept on the closed to the general public two last floors and available only by appointment and operator assisted elevator. Inside this treasure chest, there are autographs, manuscripts, letters and the first editions of rare books.

But all the rest of leather-bound tomes, maps and botanical drawings, unusual prints, century-old posters, and the entire collection of antique "printed matter," the most extensive in the city, are fully accessible and ready to admire in a classy, old-fashioned interior of wooden shelves and framed prints all over the walls (a hand-written Marcel Proust's letter among others).

There are also a miniature ship on display, and an antique style globe sphere placed in a wooden rack. They are both a good metaphor of Argo(sy)'s brave and efficient, almost 100-year-old navigation through the history of New York.

Don't judge a bookstore by its entrance

UPPER EAST SIDE

The name "Madison Avenue" just speaks for itself as a commonly recognized symbol of high-end fashion and the most expensive retail estate in the world. The enclave of "abusively" luxurious clothes, jewelry and accessories spans from 57th to 79th Streets, starting from Barney's NY, Calvin Klein and DKNY flagships, and it's filled with upscale "retail mansions," including Donna Karan, Tom Ford, YSL and Givenchy, among others. Not to mention a few "retail palaces," such as Hermes and two Ralph Lauren's stores.

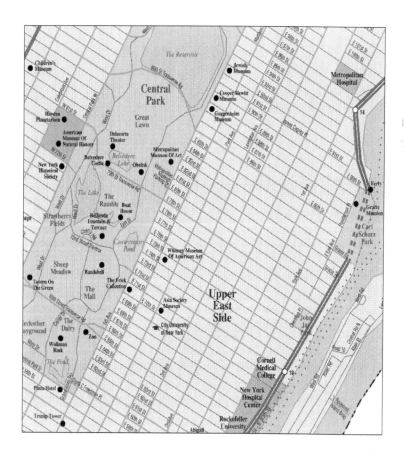

Another French invasion, this time, of Manhattan on the roof of Hermes

Bloomingdale's

1000 3rd Avenue (between 59th and 60th Streets)
www.bloomingdales.com
🚇Subway directions:
59th Street (2, 5, 6)
Lexington Avenue-59th Street (N, Q, R)
Lexington Avenue-63rd Street (F)

One of the most important reasons to visit the Blooming-dale's department store is, obviously, the iconic Big Brown Bag, exactly, as the inscription reads on it. What is far less obvious, is a long history of shopping behind that humble paper item because Bloomingdale's is the first store ever providing signature shopping bags. This big and brown bag was introduced in 1961.

However, as "words can't say it all," the store was also a pioneer in the field of "event advertising," organizing and hosting fashion galas and the first ever in-store fashion shows attracting celebrities. Being the original retail theater in New York, Bloomingdale's location at Lexington Avenue and 59th Street became not only a popular shopping destination but also a place of "seeing and being seen." In order to encourage prominent customers to visit the store every day. Bloomingdale's launched new designer's boutiques for both—already famous names and emerging ones.

The store's most notable "discoveries" are Ralph Lauren, Kenzo, Donna Karan and John Galliano, to name just a few. Furthermore, it was the original location for boutiques of Calvin Klein, YSL, and DKNY brands, which coincides with the Bloomingdale's very beginnings when other competitors, such as Lyman and Joseph, specialized in one line of products.

The Bloomingdale brothers opened, in 1872, Bloomingdale's Great East Side Bazaar selling a variety of women's fashion, creating the first genuine department store in New York. Further proof that the brothers understood the idea of volume sales better than their competitors is the policy of low prices.

This way, the clientele of the store was significantly increased by so-called "blue-collar" workers, who not only popularized shopping as mass entertainment but also evidently multiplied the owners' profits.

Today, in the art-deco historic building, the company still sticks to the great tradition of the white marble interior, offering almost every line and kind of goods, from world-famous fashion "big names" to popular brands of garment, accessories, shoes, cosmetics, luggage, and even cookware, not to mention the city's most famous treats—Magnolia Bakery cupcakes or Forty Carrots frozen yogurt.

No wonder that being the pioneer in a retailtainment business, after almost one and a half-century of operating in Manhattan, Bloomingdale's is still one of the most popular tourists' destinations in New York.

Dylan's Candy Bar

1011 3rd Avenue (at 60th Street)
www.dylanscandybar.com
🚇Subway directions:
Lexington Avenue-59th Street (5, 6, F, N, Q, R)

Ralph Lauren's emporium defines the New York style of clothing; his daughter's rainbow-colored swirl lollypops puts forward her idea of city's confectionery. She does it in her original candy store with its even more original interior and a "home-made" line of chocolates.

In this two-story temple of sweets, there is a real feast for all senses; you are welcome with an intoxicating aroma (and taste too, if you like) of chocolate, gaudy colors of the trademark lollypops, and of course, all the imaginable assortment of candies. Not only the sweets are colorful but also the walls, stands and floors of the store, so the whole place looks like a giant box of bonbons.

Dylan's Candy Bar has its own chocolate mini-factory and cafeteria, and a chocolate fountain just near the entrance.

You have a really hard time choosing among so many different sizes and colors of wrappers and boxes, and among so various sweets. By the way, you even have to choose where you want to buy—at the stands or candy bars, or at the classic glass counter filled with pralines and chocolates. And because it's not easy to choose from the diverse assortment, you can taste everything in the store cafeteria. Apart from confectionery, you can buy stationery, souvenirs, and even clothing here—to make your sweet experience more complete—in a New York way.

DKNY

655 Madison Avenue (between 60th and 61st Streets)
www.dkny.com
🚊Subway directions:
5th Avenue-59th Street (N, Q, R)
59th Street (4, 5, 6)
Lexington Avenue-59th Street (N, Q, R)

In New York, the best interior décor scenery seems to be city's "exterior"—the everyday Manhattan street life, including cityscapes, yellow cabs, and landmarks.

The same concept is applied in the LED screens coordinated with cameras following impetuous streams of passers-by.

But even better way to invite the city into a store seems to lead through...windows: wide, glass display windows opening a retail space interior for the vibrant Manhattan life with all its shapes and colors. There is just nothing more New Yorky than New York itself. And since there is nothing more New York at heart than DKNY (Donna Karan New York), the brand's three-floor flagship store on Madison Avenue has an all-glass façade and a floor-to-ceiling mirror wall inside.

This provokes an unceasing confrontation between street outside and the store activities, reflecting the one in the other and blending both the worlds into a unique urban universe.

Furthermore, this dynamic and vibrant effect is intensified

by the staircase that joins the store to the street.

Polished concrete floors with chrome and oak-wood accents, simple furniture, and a drink bar upstairs help to create an exemplary New York City specific retail space.

And, of course, DKNY offers brand "everything"—from accessories, legendary fragrances and gadgets to its newest iconic collections, and it has been doing so for more than two decades.

Barney's New York
660 Madison Avenue (at 60th Street)
www.barneys.com
🚊Subway directions:
5th Avenue-59th Street (N, Q, R)
59th Street (4, 5, 6)
Lexington Avenue-59th Street (N, Q, R)

Sarah Jessica Parker once told "Vanity Fair": "If you're a nice person, and you work hard, you get to go shopping at Barney's. It's the decent reward."

The sentence, found on the Pinterest web site, is not a lie at all. The Barney's shopping is a decent reward. It is true not only to hard-working New Yorkers but also to hard-sightseeing tourists as well.

As one of the top in quite long list of New York luxury department stores, this specific one could stand as one for all because it symbolizes all the best, upscale and pricey upper-class shopping destinations in Manhattan, including acclaimed as the most creative, inspiring and visually attractive window displays in the entire city.

Everything in Barney's seems to be just right and typical. First, the brand history with humble beginnings as a family business made from just a couple of pants and an old iron.

Second, the inner tendency for growing into a retail mammoth in the most prestigious location. Third, the target clientele, rich Manhattanites from upper-middle class, who made the place the best publicity possible. Because of celebrities shopping here, the brand made its reputation as a trendy place for all "aspiring" people, even if they have never resided at Upper East Side.

Fourth, and most importantly, for a "genuine shopping experience" because "visitors melt here into the rich and famous as well as the regular clientele from the vicinity."

The interior design is based on velvet, marble, crystal and mirrors and is exactly representative of a store fit for Manhattan millionaires.

The place fulfills collective dreams of shopping the same way rich New Yorkers, offering not only an incredibly wide selection of fashion by the best and renowned designers (prices are sky-high, however, sales make them almost affordable), but also in-store services not common in mall department stores everywhere else. So, you can ask a concierge, for assistance (the only one of this kind among city retailers), drop in a personal shopping and image studio with nationally known make-up artists and stylists, and even sate your appetite at the upscale Fred's restaurant serving "home" specialties famous in the entire city (Mark's Madison salad, to name just one).

It is also worth mentioning that the store policy accepts the "icon department store" landmark status, thus tourists are welcomed. By the way, sightseeing is really hard work, so shopping at Barney's is their decent reward. Even if it's just a window shopping.

Agent Provocateur
675 Madison Avenue (between 61st and 62nd Streets)
www.agentprovocateur.com
🚇Subway directions:
5th Avenue-59th Street (N, Q, R)
59th Street (4, 5, 6)
Lexington Avenue-63rd Street (F)

There are many kinds of libraries nowadays, such as record libraries, software libraries, and, of course, "true" libraries, the obvious ones—book libraries. So, probably, everybody has an idea how such library looks like.

How about a "hosiery library"? The answer is Agent Provocateur, located in a two-story townhouse, where you can browse through all pieces of lingerie (and buy, of course) at will. It is the one and only store of this kind in the city.

What's more, the place is enhanced by the sumptuous and elegant interior decor which consists of walls covered with mirrors and dark wood panels, Victorian club chairs, and Beardsley-style murals embellishing the staircase leading to the more intimate second floor boudoir-like arrangement with plush and silk curtains and a sleep-ready bed inside. Furthermore, there is a small greenhouse at the back of the store.

In this voluptuous interior, shopping (as AP advertises) for "classic soirée videos," lingerie, nightwear, bridal hosiery, beauty and bedding accessories and erotic toys" (a "riding" whip is hard to miss) is less than just shopping and more like visiting last century Paris gentlemen's clubs in the vicinity of the Moulin Rouge.

Even if, eventually, this unusual hosiery library turns out to be nothing more than a few upscale lingerie hangers and drawers.

Tender Buttons

143 E 62nd Street (between 3rd and Lexington Avenues)
www.tenderbuttons-nyc.com
🚇Subway directions:
Lexington Avenue-63rd Street (F)
Lexington Avenue-59th Street (N, Q, R)
50th Street (4, 5, 6)

Why in New York everything seems to be so buttoned up? It's due to housing the only shop in America devoted entirely to the buttons.

Calling this specific establishment "a store" is not quite adequate. A picturesque red brick townhouse with a big golden button as a trade sign, an antique wooden display and the interior arranged like a museum, looks rather as the old times library.

The one with a traditional cabinet directory, black and white tile floor and table lamps with green shades. Even the most precious white crows—antique, hundreds year old buttons, are hidden in the glass cases, like priceless incunabula.

The staff also display a professional librarian attitude towards the store inventory.

There is nothing unusual in the store's museum-like atmosphere since the significant portion of its stock was first owned by a button collector, which was then bought out with the entire establishment for artists' hangouts. Eventually it became a button store after it had moved to its current location.

Every one of countless types, sizes, shapes and styles of buttons has its own cardboard box, identical to the hundreds of other cardboards button boxes with a sample button and handwritten (or neatly printed) description on the surface.

All those cardboards are placed elaborately in the endless wall of similar button boxes in the order, which random logic only the librarians, I mean shopkeepers, are able to understand.

Inside the boxes, there are wooden buttons, plastic buttons, leather buttons and pearl buttons, traditional ones and novelty ones, antique buttons and artsy buttons, vintage buttons and specialty buttons—both unique and ubiquitous ones, blazer buttons (there are more than 400 types of blazer buttons in TB). You can be sure that you will be able to find any imaginable and unimaginable button in Tender Buttons—not only in its catalogue but in the store itself because it has it already in stock.

Hermes

691 Madison Avenue (at 62nd Street)
www.hermes.com
🚊Subway directions:
5th Avenue-59th Street (N, R, Q)

Having a signature Hermes scarf may be a pricey pleasure, but if you buy it in its Manhattan flagship location, the expense is surely less traumatic.

It's because of a rare opportunity of purchasing a customized silk item in the so-called "Custom Silk Corner," offering some 30 colors, several sizes and about 20 patterns of a dream accessory to choose from. However, there are more reasons to visit this particular location of the famous Paris brand in Manhattan.

The former Louis Sherry gourmet restaurant, even before its renovation in 2000, was an outstanding architectural art-deco landmark, with the original skylight top floor, and a roof glasshouse.

This French upscale company hardly complemented this already famous edifice with its accessories with signature equestrian motifs, home décor, fashion collections, and a statue of Hermes at the top of the roof. However, not the one you may think of (herald from Greek mythology).

This time, he looks like Napoleon on a white rearing steed, with two flags in his hands. It's the French part of the story, and the New York's one is a spiral staircase in the center of the store's space, with a Calder-style mobile sculpture suspended from the ceiling.

The entire interior resembles more an upscale art gallery than a retail store, and the top floor is used like one sometimes, indeed. However, even besides art exhibitions, the Hermes flagship seems to be a piece of art itself—at least, in the field of interior design.

Fivestory

18 E 69th Street (between 5th and Madison Avenues)
www.fivestory.com
🚇Subway directions:
68th Street-Hunter College (4, 6)
Lexington Avenue-63rd Street (F)
77th Street (4, 6)

Some of the stores in Manhattan can easily be mistaken for art museums. Some of them resemble contemporary Chelsea galleries. That's why, in Manhattan, the question if fashion can be considered art, and sold the same way as art—is just out of question.

So, you wouldn't be surprised trying on a pair of shoes sitting on a velvet antique sofa, looking at yourself in a crystal mirror under sparkling chandeliers, being immersed in the scent of fresh flowers, surrounded by elegant furniture, and, to complete the experience, being mesmerized by very modern photographs by Marilyn Munster. This is not common even in Manhattan.

Clair Distenfeld made it possible, who has an art background, and was an apprentice in the Metropolitan Museum of Art. She opened her first garment and accessory shop in five-story Upper-East-Side historic townhouse, and she named it, as the location suggests—"Fivestory."

That elegant simplicity of the store manifests itself not only by its name but also its assortment, consisting mostly of vanguard, unique and pricey clothing.

To make the establishment look like a Parisian boutique, its interior is highlighted by a spiral staircase with custom-made wrought-iron balustrade, walls covered with emerald green Italian velvet, black and white marble floors with graphically patterned inlays, uptown, mansion-style furniture, crystal mirrors and chandeliers, and a mezzanine garden with living plants (not so common these days) around a miniature sandstone fountain.

In such surroundings even a pair of mediocre shoes looks like an art object; however, this time it is not the case because in Fivestory, nothing is even close to mediocrity.

Ralph Lauren Men
867 Madison Avenue (at 72nd Street)
www.ralphlauren.com
🚊Subway directions:
Lexington Avenue-68th Street (6)

If by buying brand-name stuff we buy a "story and image," then the best images and stories are for sale at the Ralph Lauren Men flagship store, and they are all about old-time British gentlemen.

The image is accentuated by every detail of architecture, furniture and interior décor in the four-story mansion with the classic beaux arts façade, built over 120 years ago, previously owned by Gertrude Rhinelander, and it still remains one of the best Manhattan addresses on Madison Avenue in Upper East Side.

In the early 1980s, it underwent a thorough renovation to preserve and restore its original architectural luxuriance—black-and-white pinstriped or tweed fabric-covered walls, stuccoes, ancestral oil portraitures, leather sofas and chairs, fireplaces and solid antique furniture, and the spectacular mahogany staircase, harmoniously completed with dark wood paneling. It is reminiscent of the neoclassical style of the original edifice as a whole, and it looks like a movie setting for a sequel of "An Englishman in New York" depicting his daily activities in the Big Apple: tea parties, polo playing, kayaking, biking, cigar smoking, letter writing, working for a Wall Street corporation, drinking Starbucks coffee, and shopping in the Strand Bookstore.

The process of turning this urban mansion into the gentleman's apartment was accomplished by adding costly props: leather suitcases, leather-bound books, gym accessories, and even an old- time motorbike (it is on sale for a mere

$72,000) as well as an antique freestanding globe and a grandfather's clock.

Thanks to all those décor details, the store's space tells its story about all Ralph Lauren's signature collections—from Black Label and Purple Label to Polo and RL basics, such as cashmere sweaters and personalized iconic Polo shirts (with a monogram on demand), etc.

The tour around the Ralph Lauren store offers the same kind of experience as a visit to such Manhattan historic sites as, say, the Morris-Jumel Mansion or Merchant Home—only this one is free, and the "souvenirs" are much more practical.

Ralph Lauren Women

888 Madison Avenue (at 72nd Street)
www.ralphlauren.com
🚊Subway directions:
Lexington Avenue-68th Street (6)

Those who wonder how everyday life may look behind the doors of Manhattan urban mansions, or to be exact, palaces, they now have now an opportunity to experience that personally.

Thanks to one of the most famous American designers and the worldwide recognized symbol of American upper-middle class fashion—Ralph Lauren and his two flagships at Madison, which perfectly complete each other.

This one for women with its 38,000-square-foot space, was previously owned by Alva Vanderbilt (from those Vanderbilts, one of the richest and most prominent "new-money" families of the last century in New York).

The Vanderbilts abandoned that residence a long time ago, but their high-society spirit still reigns all over the place. The store's interior features a neoclassical style, highlighted with feminine details that create an intimate atmosphere throughout all salons on three floors. The fourth and uppermost floor is entirely filled with Ralph Lauren's Home collection.

The décor is immaculate from the floors to the ceilings, and it seems to be the interior of a rococo palace with hand-cast moldings and ornamental wrought-iron accents, stuccoes on the white walls, hand-blocked coverings and rich upholstery, parquet wood flooring, fireplaces, opulent crystal chandeliers, authentic Persian rugs, antique furniture, and a grand staircase with limestone steps and a hand-wrought metal railing, which provides access to all floors and serves as an excellent vantage point. The picture wouldn't be complete without mirrors and fresh flowers, which are almost everywhere, tastefully arranged. In such luxurious surroundings, every woman can feel like a true princess.

Besides that feeling of "princesshood," you can leave the store with a nice piece of jewelry, a signature bag (chosen from among 21 shades of crocodile leather), or anything else from Ralph Lauren's newest collection.

A few years ago, Ralph Lauren said: "It is the most romantic setting for all my women's collections, accessories and fine jewelry as well as home. It fulfills my dream of the ultimate experience for women in New York City." And he was absolutely right—the experience is amazing and unforgettable.

Annie & Company Needlepoint & Knitting

1325 Madison Avenue (between 93rd and 94th Street)
www.annieandco.com
🚆Subway directions:
96th Street (4, 6)
86th Street (4, 5, 6)

Knitta, yarn bombing, yarn bombing, yarn storming, guerrilla knitting, kniffiti, urban knitting or graffiti knitting is a graffitilike street art that employs colorful displays of knitted or crocheted yarn or fiber, and it happened to be born not in New York but in Houston, Texas in 2005. However, it is New York where the art of knitting has gained in worldwide popularity since a young Polish-born yarn artist, Agata Oleksiak "Olek," crocheted a warm pink and blue cover for the statue of the famous "Charging Bull" on Wall Street in 2010. All knitters and crocheters out there have learned that sweaters, shawls and mittens made by them can be pieces of art, not a mere hobby. Since then nobody has been confused seeing the city's benches "wearing" warm and colorful socks or park lanterns muffled in woolen scarfs. It's just art...

Let's say, it is a new tradition in New York City, and everybody is encouraged to make some personal effort to keep it going by opening yarn stores throughout the city; one of them is Annie and Company Needlepoint and Knitting.

It was established in 2002, and five years later it became to one of the largest and most complex shops of this kind in the city, fulfilling all knitting and needlepoint necessities. And, in fact, it is not only a store since a gallery is the significant part of it, among other things, offering knitting lessons.

Conveniently located in Upper East Side, near Central Park and the most visited New York museums, the store occupies three floors in the picturesque, historic brownstone; that's why, shopping here is more like visiting the house of a friend artist with his or her knitting and needlepoint studio at home.

This impression is emphasized by cozy wooden furniture consisting of wide, comfortable sofas covered with (knitted, of course) bedspreads and solid, long tables with knitting baskets, yarn hanks, and crochet supplies.

And, obviously, wool balls dispersed everywhere, as far as needlepoint and knitting works, done mostly by attendants of the continuously growing in popularity in-place workshops, especially since knitting has been considered an art. Anyway, a sweater knitted by yourself with a motif of the Empire State Building for a Christmas party—priceless!

Oh, turists, don't leave NY. If you have to...come back and have fun again

INDEX

Printed in Great Britain
by Amazon